THE
HOME & FAMILY
PROTECTION
DOG

Rommel with authors' son, Troy (age 4). Rommel's son, Ch. Kingsden's Firestorm Dallas, is shown in Chapter I with Troy (age 9). A family legacy lives on!

THE HOME & FAMILY PROTECTION DOG

Selection and Training

**Karen Freeman Duet
and George Duet**

New York

Maxwell Macmillan Canada
Toronto

Maxwell Macmillan International
New York   Oxford   Singapore   Sydney

Howell Book House
Macmillan Publishing Company
866 Third Avenue
New York, NY 10022

Maxwell Macmillan Canada, Inc.
1200 Eglinton Avenue East
Suite 200
Don Mills, Ontario M3C 3N1

Macmillan Publishing Company is part of the Maxwell Communication Group of Companies.

Library of Congress Cataloging-in-Publication Data
    Duet, Karen Freeman.
        The home and family protection dog: selection and training /
    Karen Freeman Duet and George Duet.
            p. cm.
        ISBN 0-87605-619-2
        1. Watchdogs. 2. Watchdogs—Training. I. Duet, George.
    II. Title.
    SF428.8.D84   1993   92-39466   CIP
    636.7'0886—dc20

Macmillan books are available at special discounts for bulk purchases for sales promotions, premiums, fund-raising, or educational use. For details, contact:

                    Special Sales Director
                    Macmillan Publishing Company
                    866 Third Avenue
                    New York, NY 10022

10 9 8 7 6 5 4

Printed in the United States of America

To our family, VERN, JERRE and MARC FREEMAN,
for their never-ending love and support,
our sons TROY and TRAVIS,
the light of our lives,
and our family protection dog "ROMMEL,"
who protected us with undying loyalty and devotion
to his last days.

Preface

IN TODAY'S SOCIETY, with its atmosphere of ever-increasing violence, more than ever people are mulling over their options for family protection.

One obvious alternative is the protection dog. Other options include firearms, security systems and martial arts training. Private security services are available to those willing and able to pay for it. On the whole, our security options are fairly limited.

There are many questions in the minds of those considering adding a protection dog to their family. It is our goal to educate the reader to the realities, myths, liabilities and laws concerning these dogs. The reader is taken step-by-step through the proper procedures of selecting and training the protection dog. Many of these training steps regarding puppy training, problem-solving, home manners and obedience can be applied to all dogs.

Protection steps are detailed in Chapters XIII–XVI, after which the differences in home protection dogs, European sport dogs, military, police and security K-9s are discussed.

We conclude the book with some actual stories involving protection-trained dogs.

It is our desire in writing this book to educate the potential protection dog owner on this exciting subject. We have attempted to provide a commonsense outline as a road map and guide through training.

We do not claim that these are the only methods to train a dog as there are many different styles and techniques. We simply put this forward as our method of training. We have purposely left out details with regard to how training decisions are made and specific decoy training techniques. We have also suggested throughout this book that the techniques found herein be applied under the watchful eye of a professional trainer.

If this book answers the questions of the curious, helps to spread the use of nonabusive training and/or serves as a beacon of light in the search and discovery process of the first-time owner of a protection dog, then we will have attained our goal.

During the last decade, many fine European trainers have offered their time and experience to American trainers who were seeking knowledge and new techniques. Several of these trainers are mentioned in Chapter XVII. Some of these knowledge seekers have blossomed into the best trainers in the U.S. We know these people and have seen firsthand their dedication to the art of dog training and, in some cases, breeding. Their dedication is exhibited sometimes with great sacrifice and cost, both economic and personal.

Acknowledgments

Our special thanks to Elizabeth Hardy Magers of The Quest Companies, Inc., for organizing our thoughts and polishing the manuscript.

We wish to thank the following people for their support in so many different ways.

K-9 Companions
Professional Training Staff

Lisa Spadt
DeAnn Sweeney
James Faulkner
David Macias

Steve Trachta
Pon Saradeth
Steve Schiratis

Contributing Professional
Trainers and Breeders

Stewart Hilliard
Susan Barwig
Manson and Eve Johnson
Linda and Phillip Calamia

Photographer

DeAnn Sweeney, whose spectacular photography graces the pages of this work.

Illustrator

Jim Doody, a very fine artist, whose illustrations appear in Chapter XVIII.

Contributors

Thanks to the following contributors whose achievements are acclaimed in their respective fields of expertise.

Dr. Richard W. Kobetz C.S.T. (Executive Protection Institute)
Robert Pristojkovic Esq. (Pristojkovic and Associates)
Steve Trachta (Security Force Unlimited)
Steve Schiratis (Security Force Unlimited)
Sgt. John Horton (Riverside Sheriffs)
Deputy Scott Johnson (Riverside Sheriffs K-9)
Cathi Helfer (Camp Best Friends Kennels)

Contents

Is this *your* image of a protection dog? The definition of what a protection dog should be: Loving-Loyal-Trustworthy. Troy, age 9, and Ch. Kingsden's Firestorm Dallas.

CHAPTER I

What Is a Protection Dog?

IN RECENT YEARS, a great amount of media attention—both positive and negative—has been focused on aggressive dogs. This has left the public confused as to whether owning an aggressive dog is a wise decision. Some view the matter as typical of the media's tendency to highlight acts of violence. Others believe that all "aggressive breeds" should be banned from their cities in order to protect innocent victims. However, those who are educated in the ways of dogs know that it is not the dog—but the owner—who is to blame.

Three ingredients separate vicious dogs from trained protection dogs—Breeding, Socialization and Training. If one of these is missing, you have a potentially dangerous animal.

Most dogs in the media publicity are the typical protection breeds (i.e., Rottweilers, Pit Bulls, German Shepherd Dogs and Doberman Pinschers). However, it is interesting to note that statistics show the number one and two biting dogs to be Cocker Spaniels and Poodles, respectively. This may at first surprise you. However, when you realize that these breeds are two of the most popular in the United States and are therefore the most common, it makes sense.

Small breeds do not inflict the same amount of damage as a large breed can. This is why you never hear about a Poodle biting a child in the face. The potential for publicity is much greater if that dog happens to be an aggressive breed such as a German Shepherd Dog. We are attempting to point out that the breed of dog is not the problem. The difference is in the selection, care and handling of the animal.

The family companion protection dog is generally a friendly and loving animal. This animal is balanced in nature and therefore possesses the ability to play and seek affection just like any other. What sets protection dogs apart from other dogs is heightened drives—both for defense of what is theirs and the prey drive observable in their endless willingness to chase a ball or to participate in a game of tug-of-war. These drives make it necessary that training start while the pup is young, and can also work against you if they are not molded properly.

Young protection dogs are very mouth-oriented and may chew on wood, leather or other solid items. The dog will not understand the difference between items that are valuable and those that are not. This dog will also tend to be pushy and may playfully bite at clothing, hands and/or ankles. All of these behaviors can be curbed with puppy conditioning, which is an invaluable part of your training program.

WHAT PROTECTION DOGS CAN AND CANNOT DO

A protection dog's primary function is to serve as a *deterrent*, simply by the dog's presence and aggressive behavior behind your fence, in your car and in your home. This dog's stature is enough to make the bad guy think about going somewhere easier.

It must be emphasized that you cannot consider an untrained dog to be a protection dog by virtue of breed. There are many documented cases of German Shepherd Dogs and Rottweilers, etc., allowing thieves into homes to walk off with the silver.

The two main factors that contribute to the previous example are the lack of proper selection and lack of training. A dog must be taught what to do and not to simply react by doing whatever comes naturally.

The criminal has the advantage if the dog is outdoors, by attempting to sweet-talk or intimidate the dog. If the animal is being pelted with rocks or pellets from a gun, that dog will instinctively seek cover as you would. The dog cannot fight back if the thief is on the other side of the fence.

Just as much as the outside dog has the disadvantage, the inside dog has the advantage. Inside dogs are protected from any form of abuse while surrounded by what they are protecting. In order for the intruder to get to the dog (or the home and people), the bad guy must make an opening to get through, which allows the animal to get the advantage.

We are aware of a situation where a Bullmastiff severed the hand of an intruder who was attempting to open a sliding glass door. The owner came home to discover the hand lying behind a chair next to the door. Needless to say, nothing was taken.

Not a Cure-All

The dog is not to be viewed as the end-all to security. For that matter, nothing is—not guns, alarm systems or dogs. *We believe that the more security measures you take, the more secure you are.* It is, however, true that the dog is the only one of your security options that can work as a visual deterrent, alarm system and bodyguard at the same time, while still being enjoyable when not being utilized for protection purposes.

Well-trained companion-protection dogs are a pleasure to be around. They will play with the children, go on vacations with you and do just about anything any other dogs can do as family companions. The difference is that they have been taught an extra responsibility, that of family protector. The dog knows not to allow strangers to come in uninvited, but if the dog is told it is "Okay," then—and only then— will visitors be allowed to enter.

The dogs also know to come to the aid of any family member. If commanded to apprehend an intruder, they will do so by either a bark and hold command, or will bite to hold when necessary, but will release and guard on command. The family protection dog has received strict Obedience training and is controlled in action.

After painting a picture of what they should be like, let's talk about what they cannot be expected to do.

The first thing you should know is that dogs do not have the ability to reason. Their responses are primarily instinctual and conditioned responses. This is why it is imperative for a dog to practice training under the conditions likely to be encountered. Understanding the dog's lack of reasoning is important for both safety and liability. Even though an animal may have all of this wonderful training and ability, it is up to you to determine when and how the dog uses it. Bad judgment could get both of you in serious trouble.

For example, someone swinging a baseball bat too close to you or slapping you on the back in a friendly but forceful manner could trigger the animal's conditioned response, so you have to be careful to

3

"read" your dog and simply say it is "okay." Do not expect your companion protection dog to be "Lassie" or "Rin Tin Tin."

A woman once called us and said that she wished to purchase a dog for family protection. She wanted to put the dog in the front yard with her two very young daughters, just in case someone tried to abduct them. This may not seem unreasonable at first, until you realize what the woman would be expecting from the dog and the risk that she would be taking. The potential for disaster here is extremely high. She would be expecting her dog to reason out the good guys from the bad guys. What if one of her daughters was to fall and cry out, and a well-meaning neighbor rushed over to comfort the child? Would the dog know that this is a good guy? Suppose a serviceman came onto the property to make a delivery or read a meter, would the dog know that this person is a good guy? The answer is a resounding "NO" in both cases.

The front yard of a home is a public place and a dog has no business being off leash without being under complete control of an immediate handler. This is true even of an untrained or nonaggressive dog.

TRAINED VS. UNTRAINED

Many people have stated that they do not want to protection train their Rottweilers, German Shepherd Dogs, etc., because they are afraid of the liability, or they believe the dogs will be aggressive enough "naturally." While a protection dog is not for everyone, in both cases there is a great deal of misconception and misunderstanding at work. In reality, a properly trained protection dog is taught when it is appropriate to be aggressive and when it is not. Also 50 percent of the training is based on Obedience and ceasing aggression on command. The likelihood of any dog being a greater liability *if trained properly* is a myth.

If the training is improper and does not stress Obedience and the "Out" command, or the command to stop aggression, you will have a greater liability. This is why choosing your trainer is so important. (See Chapter III.)

The untrained dog is an unpredictable dog. Assuming any breed to be naturally protective is dangerous. We firmly believe that you should never rely on your dog's ability to protect you unless the dog has been trained to do so. This can go either of two ways. Since there is not the advantage of condition through training, the dog is left to

4

instinctual responses—fight or flight. Seventy-five percent of untrained dogs will run.

On the other hand, there are dogs who become known as the neighborhood bully, who have learned that they can scare people and there is nothing you can do about it. This is where you have your greatest liability with any breed—owning a dog with no obedience and no control. It is bad enough to have an uncontrollable small dog running around biting people. However, if the dog is a 130-pound hulk, it is a very serious and potentially lethal matter. In our opinion, every dog—large or small—should have basic Obedience training. This would prevent countless injuries and potentially save lives.

The owner's responsibility toward a dog cannot be overemphasized. It is the owner and not the dog who will dictate whether the dog is dangerous or under control. Remember, most dogs have the same mental and emotional state as a three-year-old child. It is because of this that they must be taught and managed properly. It is the owner's ultimate responsibility to keep the dog under control at all times. When you hear of a dog-bite case, whether it is a police K-9 or a neighborhood dog, the question must be asked, "Where was the owner?" With regard to a police K-9, "Did the handler have control?" "Did the officer use the K-9 properly?" *For every trained dog, there should be a trained handler who controls the animal's actions.* Therefore, ownership of a protection breed should not be entered into without forethought.

To conclude, it is not the family protection dog that bites people on the streets without provocation. It is the untrained, unkempt, mentally and/or physically abused dog that exhibits this type of behavior. Many have been tied most of their lives, leaving them frustrated and vicious.

The family protection dog is a carefully bred, carefully selected, carefully trained and carefully handled animal. He or she is a loved and respected family member, and upon death is mourned. This loss leaves the family feeling vulnerable and unprotected, as they are used to the loyalty, comfort and security the animal provides. Once you have had the pleasure of owning a family protection dog, you will never be without one.

What if this were your dog but not your baby?

CHAPTER II

Liabilities and Legalities

LIABILITY is a serious consideration with regard to ownership of a protection dog. Typically, one pictures a protection dog as a snarling mouth full of teeth. In one respect, this is precisely why protection dogs are useful, because the psychological aspect is enough of a deterrent. On the other hand, it is also one reason why many people fear ownership of a protection dog.

The dog training occupation dictates that we must educate the public-at-large as to the realities of protection dog ownership so that accurate lines can be drawn between myth and misconception versus reality. We can safely state that very few *unwarranted* attacks are carried out by **TRAINED** protection dogs.

The next time that you hear about an attack carried out by a protection type of dog, ask, "Was it trained?" This is a critical point, as many people classify a protection dog as such simply by breed. Many others will refer to their German Shepherd Dogs as police dogs although there is no correlation with actual police service or training.

Often we are asked if there is an increased danger of liability in owning a protection dog. Our answer is an emphatic "Yes!" It stands to reason that ownership brings with it both responsibilities and liabilities. It is also true that having a swimming pool in your backyard carries with it more liabilities than not owning one. The owner of a car, pool, weapon or a protection dog must take full responsibility for ownership. Legally, you have the same responsibilities with your dog as you would have with anything you own that could prove harmful to others.

It is not legal, nor is it safe, to allow your dog to run around off your property without a leash. If your dog causes injury to another person, animal or property, you are responsible. Your dog must be housed behind a fence that is tall enough to protect against small children or unwanted guests wandering into the dog's area. It is law in some states that warning signs be posted at all potential entrances to a property where a protection dog is housed.

Simply stated, if you cannot handle this responsibility, you should not own a dog. A person who cannot be, or who refuses to be, responsible for a dog's actions should definitely not own a protection dog.

PROPER MANAGEMENT

In general, you should treat your dog as you would a two- to three-year-old child. You are responsible for the dog's safety, and actions as well. You would not permit your two-year-old to wander down the street alone for safety reasons, so why would you let your dog do the same?

There are many reasons why people claim that they can't keep their dogs in the yard:

- The yard is too large to fence.
- The fence has holes in it.
- The dog digs out under the fence.
- The dog chews through the fence.
- The kids let the dog out.
- The gardener lets the dog out.

There is one simple answer to the aforementioned dilemmas— the dog run. The dog run—an area approximately 5 feet by 20 feet with 6-foot-high sides, a top (if necessary) and a cement base—is all the dog needs when not supervised by you.

How can your dog protect you from inside a dog run? A better question is, how will a dog who runs away or is killed by a car protect you? To find out how you can teach your dog to live in the yard without having to rely on a dog run, see Chapter VI (Confinement Conditioning).

LICENSING

Most cities or counties require licensing of dogs that live within their boundaries. Licenses help to identify dogs that are picked up on the street and taken to the local animal control facility.

You can obtain a license from your local police department or animal control facility. You will be required to show proof of a rabies vaccination and pay a nominal licensing fee. Animal control agencies often go door-to-door to check the number of dogs housed on the premises and to ensure that each animal has a license. You will be fined if you cannot show proof of licensing or if your dog is ever picked up by animal control. Laws regarding dogs are not consistent in every state or county. Therefore, it is important that you understand the laws that pertain to your particular area.

Limits on the Number of Dogs

Many areas limit the number of dogs that can be housed on a property, and generally this varies between two and four dogs per resident. In some areas, you can purchase a kennel license that will allow you to house more than the standard number. Usually this will be restricted to people within rural areas with property large enough to accommodate the dogs. Restrictions will also apply as to how the dogs are housed and how many neighbors you have. Copies of animal-related laws can be acquired at your local animal control office, health or police department.

LAWS THAT PROTECT DOGS

There are laws that exist to protect dogs themselves. For instance, California law requires that all dogs riding in the back of open pickups be restrained in order to keep them from falling or being thrown out of a vehicle by accident. It is also illegal in many areas to leave dogs in vehicles on hot days, as many dogs have died of heatstroke in this manner. These laws are good because they help to prevent unwitting owners from harming their dogs.

We believe that a dog should be required to pass basic Obedience training before one year of age to receive a license. This would cut down on a number of problems with loose and unruly dogs. After all, there are Obedience courses that fit everyone's budget and time requirements.

BREED BANNING

As of August 12, 1991, it became an offense to breed, sell, exchange, advertise or abandon a Pit Bull in the United Kingdom. This ban also affected the Tosa Inu, Dogo Argentino and the Fila Brasileiro—all fighting breeds. However, this does not mean that every dog of these breeds residing in the U.K. or elsewhere is dangerous.

Many people wonder where this might stop. Is the Rottweiler, German Shepherd Dog or Doberman Pinscher next? Isn't saying every dog of a certain breed is dangerous somewhat like saying every person of a certain race is dangerous? Would it not be wiser to ask where lies the owner's responsibility for the dog's actions? It seems to us that to require controlled breeding and a certain amount of training would be a more sensible approach to this problem.

IS A DOG CONSIDERED A DEADLY WEAPON?

Under California law (Penal Code Section 245a), a deadly weapon or instrument is defined as anything that could produce, and is likely to produce, death or great bodily harm. The court has stated that "In a given situation, a dog may well come within this definition. If an inanimate object, such as a pillow, a straight pin imbedded in an apple and a razor blade may be found to be a deadly weapon or instrument within the meaning of Section 245, certainly a dog which is trained to viciously attack a human or which has a known propensity to do so when ordered by its handler should also be considered."

The court did, however, indicate that each case should be judged on its own particular circumstances. The court concluded with these words: "Depending upon the circumstances of each case, a dog trained to attack humans on command, or one without training that follows such a command and which is of sufficient size and strength relative to its victim to inflict death or great bodily injury, may be considered a deadly weapon."

This ruling proves the amount of responsibility involved in owning a protection dog. It should be understood that a protection dog is only to be used for defensive purposes.

Traditionally, a police dog has been considered low on the scale of force. In fact, the dog could be used before a baton. This is because a bite typically would result in a few puncture wounds that could be

This is an unsafe situation.

A pet carrier makes transportation safer.

easily treated, whereas a blow with a baton or a bullet would be more likely to cause serious bodily injury or death.

YOUR RIGHTS AS A DOG OWNER

As an owner, you have rights too. You have the right to defend yourself and your family against attacks. You may decrease your liability if your dog is kept on a leash or confined safely on your property. You can show proof that your dog should be absolved of blame should an unfortunate instance arise. It is necessary for you to understand your responsibility to your dog and to others and therefore prevent potential liabilities.

If this were a perfect world with perfect people living in it, it would not be necessary to make decisions about how to best protect ourselves and our families. We all know this is not the case. With the high crime rate, many people are looking at their options, which include:

- Firearms
- Alarm systems
- Personal protection K-9

The more deterrents you possess, the better, as long as you are responsible enough to handle the safety requirements and the training involved with each of your options.

It is unfortunate that you cannot guarantee your safety even if you possess every option available to you. You can, however, stack the odds in your favor. If you love dogs and are quite sure that you can handle the responsibilities that go with ownership, the personal protection K-9 may be right for you.

A LAWYER'S POINT OF VIEW

Robert Pristojkovic is an attorney who is very familiar with K-9 law. He has worked with many local protection trainers and police officers and is a member of the Board of Directors of the Humane Society in Riverside, California.

"The ownership of a personal protection dog carries large responsibilities. The dog, while highly trained, is an animal which must be tightly controlled. Its curiosity and energy, if unsupervised, can create situations where property damage, injury or death can occur.

"As one familiar with the law, I am well aware of the laws which control these types of dogs. Laws in various jurisdictions control ownership of dogs in general and protection dogs in particular. Owners, or potential owners, of these dogs should check with their local municipalities and their state laws to conform to the guidelines laid out by the relevant authorities.

"In general, common sense must be used. The dogs must be confined and signs indicating their presence on the property must be posted. Furthermore, strangers' access to the dog's location should be minimized and/or eliminated.

"You must remember that the law may treat your protection dog as a dangerous weapon. In general, the law states that you can meet force with like force. In other words, you may encounter some problems if your dog is used improperly. A *general rule* is that you can only use force to *protect yourself, not your property*. In other words, use of the dog for personal protection may be viewed more favorably than using the dog to protect your VCR or television set.

"Also, use of the dog must be calculated. If for instance a thirteen year-old, 115-pound boy breaks into your house and you are a thirty-year-old, 225-pound man trained in martial arts, use of the dog may be deemed inappropriate.

"While not intending my statements to be an endorsement of these dogs nor a condemnation of their ownership, I strongly encourage serious protection dog owners to check local and state governments to learn of the rules applying to ownership of these dogs.

"Ultimately, ownership of a protection dog requires much more than an untrained dog. You must be willing to control the dog like a drill sergeant trains troops. At the same time, you must show it love and affection to further the bonding process. Above all, you must *never* forget that your favorite companion is dangerous if not controlled. When you look into your dog's eyes, realizing how wonderful the companionship and friendship is, do not forget that strength and power behind your canine's loving, slobbering kiss. Remember, you have assisted in breaking through the domestication and, therefore, you are responsible for the dog's actions, life and your own protection. The canine is simply an extension of yourself.''

Intensity

Enthusiasm

Affection

14

CHAPTER III

Selecting Your Trainer and Training Program

BEFORE you select your puppy or dog, it is wise to select a trainer who will become your dog's teacher, mentor and friend in the coming months. Actually this is quite a logical step since your trainer will be able to provide you with leads on breeders and/or importers. There are excellent trainers who also are breeders and/or importers.

Finding a reputable trainer is the most difficult part of the process of creating your finished product—a loving, well-trained addition to your family. It is essential that you take the necessary time and "do your homework" in this area. Keep in mind that a bad trainer can be worse than no trainer at all. This person has the potential to ruin your dog's spirit or promote aggression without control.

WHAT QUALITIES ARE EXHIBITED BY A GOOD TRAINER?

A good trainer is not necessarily the one who has the largest or the most impressive (from the outside) operation, or the one who drives a fancy car. While these trappings are symbolic of success, they do not necessarily guarantee a trainer's integrity or subject knowledge.

Remember, there is a vast difference between a good trainer and a good salesperson.

It is often very confusing for the novice to know which qualities to look for in a trainer. This is frequently compounded by the various philosophies of trainers and breeders you will encounter. As with anything, talk is cheap and it does not train dogs. The best way to differentiate between trainers' qualities is to watch dogs actually being trained by a particular trainer and to observe the "finished dogs." This will cost you nothing but the investment of time, which will prove to be well worth it. You also will find this process extremely educational in nature.

OBSERVATION—ASKING QUESTIONS

The trainer should have no reservations to showing you the kennels (all of them and not just one) and to letting you view the training process. Feel free to ask any questions that come to mind.

When a trainer demonstrates dogs for you, you should ask if:

- The dog was imported, and if so, at what age
- The animal was trained before coming to this trainer
- Any further training has been given to the dog since acquired by the trainer

Unfortunately, when you watch a demonstration of a trainer's techniques, you can never be 100 percent certain that you are seeing this particular trainer's training. This is because many dogs that are imported already have training and/or titles. A simple analogy demonstrates this fact—the trainer is "driving the car," but did not create it. There is a big difference, as some trainers simply do not possess the knowledge to build a dog from a puppy up.

It is imperative that you understand the preceding if you choose to start with a puppy. This is why we believe in building the dogs ourselves. It helps us to become acquainted with the dog through and through.

Remember to be aware of the fact that trainers often have tight schedules. An hour of their time should be sufficient to see what is necessary unless, of course, you are invited to remain.

While you are there, take note of the following:

- The cleanliness of the facilities.
- Is there enough kennel space so that the dogs can move about freely and stay away from their waste?

Professional trainers should own a large selection of training equipment to aid you and your dog in training.

- Is there adequate shelter from the elements (i.e, rain, snow, etc.)?
- Is there fresh water in the water buckets?
- What seems to be the prevailing attitude of the dogs in the kennel?
- What kind of food is fed to the dogs and what are the scheduled feeding times? (In a training kennel, the dogs should be fed just before dark when it is cool. They should never be fed prior to or right after training.)

While observing a training session, note the dogs' general attitude. It should appear that the animals are having fun learning. Dogs possess different personality traits and temperaments; however, if you notice an overall fear or shyness on the part of the dogs, the place should be avoided. Be on the lookout for general control with both the Obedience and the protection training. And remember, if you are watching a young dog in training, you cannot expect perfection. However, you can tell if an animal is being harshly treated or if there is a lack of control in the methods being taught.

PROTECTION TRAINING

If you see group protection training (when more than three dogs are being worked at a time), avoid it.

Older dogs should be worked alone. At times, a young dog can learn from watching or being worked next to a more experienced dog, The group work that we are suggesting to avoid is the type where novice owners are holding their dogs in groups of six or more, while a decoy agitates each one. *This is a dangerous practice and one that should be avoided at all costs.* It teaches group frenzy and does nothing to promote control. It also poses a danger to the dogs and the people for accidental bites.

Why is this practice going on? For MONEY, pure and simple. A trainer can make a quick profit by charging $10 per dog per session and taking in $60 to $200 for an hour's work that consists of agitating dogs into a frenzy. Some owners get a cheap thrill out of seeing their dogs become aggressive, and it is likely they will return for more the following week.

What does this teach? Because there is no method to the madness, the dog learns only to become an aggressive bully. An animal who is protection trained learns to turn *on and off* on command. This dog must learn to become aggressive on command and to do so even if being sweet-talked. A protection dog must also learn to turn off (or cease aggression) even if an aggressive situation presents itself. A finished dog must be agitated and controlled in the home environment. These are the desired behaviors. They cannot be accomplished in hour-long group classes at $10 per dog.

What you should be looking for is a positive course that spans at least the first two years of the dog's life. If you were to teach just general obedience and deterrent training, this could be accomplished by eighteen months of age. The course you take should be private one-on-one training either done in the home or a combination of in-kennel and in-home training. A portion should always take place in the animal's home.

The following questions can help you find the best professionals.

- How long have you been in business?
- How did you get into the business?
- What type of training background do you come from?
- Are you city or state licensed?
- Can I watch a training session and ask questions?
- Do you train all breeds?
- Do you specialize in a certain area or breed?
- Do you continue to learn from others (i.e., attend seminars, read, have a foreign exchange)?
- Do you have references I can call?

A friendly and knowledgeable training staff and a professional facility is what you are looking for.

- Do you have a contract that guarantees your training?
- Do you offer maintenance training?
- Do you have a video (or can I watch a live demonstration of a finished dog)?

The length of time in business is particularly important because it can provide you with "insurance" that your trainer will be in business long enough for you to finish your dog and, ideally, complete the maintenance period. It also lets you know that a new trainer is not going to make first-time mistakes with your dog.

BACKGROUND CHECK

It will be both interesting and informative to discover how the trainer got into business and what the person's training background is.

- Come from a family of dog lovers?
- Get into dog sport and turn it into a career?
- Read a book and decide to be a trainer?
- Most importantly, is the person in it for the *dogs* or the *dollars*. There is a big difference.

There are many types of backgrounds that you may come in contact with. Among them, the individual:

- Apprenticed under a professional trainer
- Was employed by a kennel and thus experienced on-the-job training
- Learned during military service
- Learned by participation in a dog sport club (AKC, Schutzhund, Ring Sport, etc.)
- Was a police K-9 handler
- Was self-taught either through books, tapes, etc. (very undesirable)

Every way of learning has its advantages and disadvantages. The problem with a trainer being so indoctrinated with one method for one job is not being flexible enough to change training philosophy for a different job. For instance, it is very different to train an animal for military or police service than it is for family protection. Yes, the same skills are taught. However, the family dog must become socialized with a larger number of people. Problems such as digging and chewing must be solved because the dog does not live in a kennel. Therefore, the dog must be trained in the home (on his turf so to speak), and the dog's owners must be properly trained.

What you are ideally looking for is someone who is training for realistic situations and not sport. Although Schutzhund and Ring Sport (European Dog Sport) skills can be utilized in the teaching of protection dogs, the application is different. You do not want to spend your money with a trainer who is a dog sport person who will train your dog "on the side." The dog will learn, but is much more likely to work like a *sport* dog and be equipment-oriented rather than person-oriented—the way a good home dog should be.

The trainer should be able to produce a license. If you have any questions, call the licensing agent, animal control, the city, consumer affairs, the Better Business Bureau, etc. Any trainer who is a professional should have no problem taking you on a tour of the entire kennel, letting you watch the dogs work, and should actually take pleasure in the process, as long as you are respectful of time.

BREED PREFERENCES

For obvious reasons, it is important to ask whether a trainer specializes in a certain type of training or breed. For instance, if you own a Rottweiler and the trainer has an aversion to them for whatever reason, this is certainly not the trainer for your dog. Seek out a trainer who willingly wants to work with your dog and has extensive experience with the breed. Also, if the trainer is an avid Obedience competitor, this person may not be qualified to handle protection.

Dog training is constantly changing. You cannot expect to get to a point, stop and decide that you know everything. The best trainers readily seek out other professionals to learn from—breeders, veterinarians, equipment companies and other trainers including foreign trainers. The Europeans possess a great wealth of information and the foremost American trainers have learned a few things from them throughout the years.

DOS AND DON'TS

Always call a trainer's references. Believe it or not, we have heard of trainers whose references, when called, said they could not stand a particular trainer and that they could not comprehend why this person would give their name out as a reference. It is best not to assume that all references are preset to sing a trainer's praises.

Also, when considering a trainer:

1. Secure a copy of the contract and carefully read every word of it.
2. Pay the fee as the services are rendered.
3. Do not agree to pay in advance for a year or two of training. Pay as you go programs give you more leverage and insurance. You should never have to pay for more than the course you are taking at the time.
4. Check to see that maintenance is offered. Family protection dogs should be worked on a regular basis.

Finally, you should be able to watch a dog in training and a finished dog. The dog in training will help you to judge how your dog will be treated. The finished product will give you an idea of what to expect. If you are not pleased with one or the other, go elsewhere.

WHAT METHODS ARE AVAILABLE

In general, you will find that there are three different training methods available to you. This can be confusing because the trainer may not describe a method by name. With the descriptions provided here, you can figure out for yourself by asking two basic questions:

- What methods of correction are used?
- What forms of praise and motivation are used?

The three methods are as follows:

1. "Schmooze" training or the "no choke chain" method

This method is one where the negative behavior is ignored and the positive is reinforced primarily with food. These trainers usually believe that choke chains are cruel. This can be compared to "Dr. Spock" training. The dog is asked to perform a specific task and then rewarded with food, or called away from a bad behavior and rewarded with food. The problem here is apparent. No discipline is involved in this method. While it is a desirable method for puppies (eight to sixteen weeks of age), an aggressive or stubborn dog will soon tire of this game. There will be times when a dog is not hungry, or will be preoccupied with something more interesting.

We have seen dogs with dominant personalities become more aggressive after the use of this type of training simply because the owner patronized the animal at every turn. This very permissive method for dogs is the same as if you tried rewarding your children's good behavior with candy, but never corrected their bad behavior.

2. Mutual respect method

This is the method that we firmly believe in and practice. It is one where the goal is to have a happy working dog and one that also respects your authority. The corrections here are by two means—the use of a training collar (not to choke the dog) by a *quick jerk and release* and instinctual corrections using the dog's senses (hearing, taste, smell) to indicate that an action is wrong.

On the plus side, a positive action will be rewarded with anything that motivates the dog (i.e., praise, a toy or food). Most trainers will try to stick to praising the dog if at all possible. Realistically, people don't always carry around food or a dog toy.

The majority of all competitive working dogs are trained by this method. Using this method, you can keep spirits up while making sure that the dog will follow through with a command, even if the dog is "not in the mood" to do so.

3. Aversion training

Aversion training is the exact opposite of "schmooze" training. It is training by negative reinforcement. The prevailing philosophy is "do it or you will be hurt." Shock collars are the typical device used in this type of training. It is thought of by some as a quick fix to training because the dog learns quickly.

The problem is the noticeable decline in the spirit of dogs who are subjected to this type of training. The distinct possibility exists that the dog will realize that the shock comes from the collar. The training over time will fall apart when the collar is no longer used.

Forced retrieving is another form of aversion training—teaching the dog to receive pain, either to the ear or to the toes, and when the dumbbell is held in the dog's mouth, the pain stops. We have seen trainers literally let dogs scream from aversion training methods. Needless to say, it is sad to see the confusion in the face of a dog who does not know what to do, but desperately wants the pain to end. It is much easier to teach a dog to retrieve as a puppy and never have to resort to these methods.

Aversion training can be applied with a choke chain as well, by the trainer who loses patience with a dog who will not do something and the trainer hangs the dog until he or she gives in.

Poison-proofing a dog and anti-snake training does require shock. However, the aversion training can get out of hand. The only time aversion training is necessary or acceptable in our opinion is to protect the dog or the owner from physical harm (i.e., poisoning, snakebites, vicious attacks, chronic fence jumping or car chasing). Even then, all other possible methods of training should be attempted first.

Avoid trainers who use aversion training as a basic method. Your dog's spirit will suffer for it and neither you nor the dog will have a positive training experience.

GROUP CLASSES, IN-HOME/IN-KENNEL TRAINING

There are three types of training available to you and your dog. As a rule of thumb, the more time the trainer spends on a one-on-one basis with you and your animal, the more expensive the training will be.

At the same time, you cannot necessarily judge quality by price. If you check around, you will come up with a ballpark figure for each type of training in your area.

Group Classes

In general, group classes are the least expensive and the least effective.

These are often run by city parks and recreation departments, kennels or pet stores. They are the least effective because they have little or no private involvement with you and your dog. Everything is done in a group and you must follow step-by-step in order to keep up.

If your dog is unruly or aggressive, you will be asked to leave the class. The cost is generally $50 to $195 for classes five to ten weeks in length. Usually no home manners or problem-solving is discussed, just your basic five commands: Heel, Sit, Stay, Come and Down. Some exceptional dogs and people may do well. However, due to a high dropout rate, we usually see only 30 to 50 percent effectiveness. If your goal is to train your dog for family protection, choose a private form of training to ensure quality.

Any good trainer will want to see your dog's previous training before starting protection work. Your dog will be ready to start if the five basics on and off leash are understood and performed well.

Group classes are good for a home dog that is mild-mannered or for an Obedience-title–minded person who already understands basic training. For these reasons, a group class also is good for socialization. However, it can be considered more the icing on the cake than the cake itself. (Cost estimate: $50–$195 per course)

In-Home Training

In-home training is accomplished entirely in the dog's home. There are some definite advantages to this type of training. For one, handling the dog's problems that occur in the home teaches manners where the dog lives while working around the typical neighborhood distractions, etc.

The main drawback is the potential lack of socialization. A dog who remains at home and never has to deal one-on-one with strangers may become fear aggressive or shy with strangers. It always is a good idea to leave your dog in the care of a trustworthy person once or twice during the first year of life, so that it will not be so traumatic later on.

One of the main reasons that in-home training sometimes fails is the lack of consistency and repetition on the owner's part. This is one very important aspect of in-home training. In-home training is a process of the trainer training the owner to train the dog. Dogs and owners must do their homework daily for this to be successful.

People who are employed eight to twelve hours a day are advised to go with a combination of an in-kennel and in-home course, in order to have the first and hardest part done for them. (Estimated cost: $395–$595 per course)

In-Kennel/In-Home Combination

The first question that usually comes to mind when in-kennel training is mentioned is ''Will the dog respond to the owner after being trained by someone else?'' The answer is yes and no. The dog will respond to whoever has a working relationship with that animal. The dog must be conditioned to work in a familiar environment. Therefore a kennel training program that begins and ends at the kennel is not a good program.

The best program of all is the in-kennel/in-home combination. This allows the dog to be taught by a professional. In phase two of the training, the dog and the owner are taught together at the owner's home. (Estimated in-kennel/in-home training cost with board: $600–$800 per course)

There are many advantages to this method:

1. The dog is started by a trainer who is not making novice mistakes with the dog.
2. The dog is socialized to new people, animals and environments.
3. The dog is worked around the distractions of other animals, smells and people.
4. The owner can start with a dog that is trained, and can concentrate on learning rather than on teaching the dog something the owner is just learning also.
5. Owner time and repetition is cut in half. Although working daily with the dog for the next few weeks is vitally important, with in-kennel/in-home training, the hardest portion of the initial conditioning has been accomplished. Twenty minutes per day for the next three to four weeks is all that is necessary.

BOARDING, GROOMING AND VETERINARY SERVICES

Hopefully, your trainer will own or be associated with a respectable boarding kennel and groomer. This will make the process of boarding or grooming the dog easier because your dog will be familiar with the surroundings and the staff.

It is vital that you inspect ALL of the facilities before you allow your dog to be kenneled. The kennels should be clean and safe. Clean means free of dirt and reasonably free of waste. Stainless-steel (or similar sturdy material) water buckets should be provided. Safe means free of protruding objects and that secure and adequate shade and shelter are provided.

Grooming services are necessary at least monthly on some protection breeds such as the Bouvier des Flandres. To keep a Bouvier coat in top condition, the dog should be groomed at least once every two weeks.

It is recommended that the pup learn to be groomed from the start. Do not wait until your pup is a young adult to experience boarding or grooming, as the stress will be greater when a dog is older. Any dog who grows up with these services as a part of life will have an easier time when you go on vacation or take the dog for regular grooming.

A professional kennel should be clean and sanitary. Shown: Camp Best Friends, indoor kennel facility in Yorba Linda, California.

A Professional View

Cathi Helfer is the owner and operator of Camp Best Friends, a full-service boarding, grooming and training service (associated with K-9 Companions Dog Training Co.) with locations in West Los Angeles and Yorba Linda, California.

Ms. Helfer learned animal husbandry while working with famous wild animal trainer Ralph Helfer, who happens to be her brother. The two raised lions, elephants, orangutans, chimpanzees and other exotic animals at their exotic animal ranch, The Gentle Jungle.

The Helfers revolutionized the training of exotics with "affection training," which lead to their success in the movie industry with many motion picture and television parts, including *Tarzan* with Bo Derek, *Any Which Way You Can* starring Clint Eastwood, *Gentle Ben, Clarence, the Cross-Eyed Lion, Daktari* and many more.

We asked Ms. Helfer what she would suggest to dog owners who are looking for a home away from home for their dogs. She stated that a little time spent asking questions and observing/inspecting facilities can make a big difference. You should be looking for someone to take care of your animals who has an "extended family mentality." This way your dog will feel as though the kennel owner is like family when you are away.

Ms. Helfer also suggested that you examine the runs. They should be of sufficient size with sleeping areas and fresh water. Adequate shelter is a must. Ms. Helfer advises that a kennel should have an "open door policy," and that you should have the opportunity to see all of the kennel runs. You should not be turned away or shown an example of the run your dog will be in. Even an older kennel can be kept clean with a little effort. Cleanliness is so very important.

With regard to a groomer, Ms. Helfer recommends that you meet the groomer who will groom your dog and discuss any special needs the dog has. You should have an understanding with regard to how the dog is to be treated.

The dog can be groomed with a soft muzzle if necessary. Drop in from time to time and observe the groomer with your dog or others. Get a feeling for the relationship the groomer has with the dogs.

You should be aware of the potential health problems of your breed and work with your vet to minimize your dog's susceptibility to these problems.

Veterinary medicine is constantly changing. Find out if your vet keeps up with the latest techniques. Ms. Helfer stresses that you should inquire as to whether there are breeds that the vet does not care to treat.

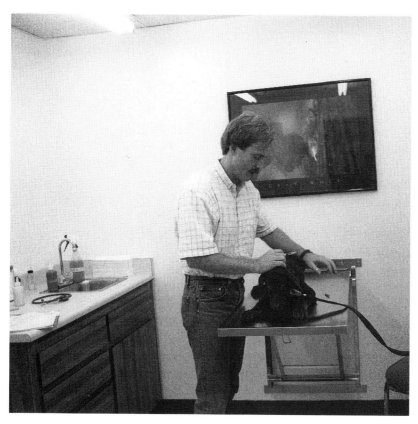
Make sure your veterinarian is comfortable with protection breeds.

For instance, if you take your Rottweiler to a vet who is afraid of this breed, neither party will be comfortable. The dog will sense the apprehension, and become nervous and possibly aggressive because of this apprehension.

DOG TRAINERS

Boarding Kennels—Groomers—Veterinarians
Interview Check List

_____ How long have they been in business?
_____ What is their philosophy (re: care and handling of the animals)?
_____ How clean is the facility?
_____ What is their attitude toward you?

_____ What is their attitude toward your breed of dog?
_____ Are they afraid of protection-type breeds?
_____ What are the dogs fed? How much? When?
_____ Do they have access to fresh water?
_____ Are the dogs ever tranquilized or given any type of drugs without owner approval? (Kennel or groomer)
_____ Do they know how to groom your breed? (Groomer)
_____ Where did they go to veterinary school? (Vet)
_____ Do they have an in-house laboratory or do they have to send tests out? (Vet)
_____ Do they have an open inspection policy? (Kennel)
_____ Indoor kennel—ventilation system?
_____ Outdoor kennel—shade and shelter?

CHAPTER IV

Selecting Your Breeder and Choosing a Source

ONCE you have made the decision to purchase a dog for family protection, there are a number of steps that you should take:

- Choose a trainer.
- Seek out the advice of your trainer first. Trainers can be very helpful in directing you to a breeder or importer with an excellent reputation.
- With the help of your trainer, you should have a basic understanding of what qualities make a good breeder or importer.

BREEDING

Good breeders know what they are breeding for, and they have an ideal picture in their minds of the traits they are trying to create in their puppies. For example, if there is a minor fault in the female, a male will be selected to offset the fault. You should insist on seeing the dam. If it is not possible to see the sire, request a video or still photos.

Puppies' pedigrees should be available for your inspection. The Orthopedic Foundation for Animals (OFA) Certificates of both the sire and dam also should be available. OFA documentation certifies that the animal is free of hip dysplasia—largely a genetic defect and very prevalent in German Shepherd Dogs and Rottweilers as well as other large breeds.

Ask what diseases are common to the breed. Do not hesitate to inquire whether the pups have been checked and/or immunized for these. For instance, parvovirus is deadly to Rottweilers and Dobermans. It is now common practice for some breeders to give shots to Rottweilers every seven to ten days until the dogs reach four months of age.

Von Willebrand's Disease (VWD), a bleeding disorder, is common to Dobermans and some other breeds. Brood bitches and stud dogs should be tested for VWD. Dobermans and Rottweilers also can experience thyroid problems. They should be tested for these as well.

One must also keep in mind that just because a dog comes from champion lines, this is no guarantee a dog will be a good protection dog. Champions are bred for beauty which may have little to do with working ability. Proof of a dog's working ability is a must.

You can see this in two ways:

1. Watch the sire and dam work, preferably in person or by video.
2. Ask to see the dog's working titles and score book. If the dog or bitch has been titled in European sport, they most likely will produce the same drives in their puppies.

Good breeders will be willing to provide you with the strengths and the weaknesses of their lines. Keep in mind that all dogs have faults, and good breeders recognize this fact and try to breed away from the faults. Your breeder should sell you a puppy with a contract that guarantees the puppy to be free of a debilitating disease at the time of sale, or disqualifying faults (i.e., those that would prevent you from showing or breeding) for the first two years of life. There should be some form of compensation if the above does occur, i.e., money back, another puppy, or second pup sold at a lesser price.

ENVIRONMENT AND THE BREEDER

Take a good long look at where your puppy has been living. Is it clean and free of dirt, trash, flies, etc.? The pups should be born inside and should be kept there at least until their eyes open. This is because puppies cannot regulate their own body temperatures for several weeks and they can die if they become chilled or overheated. Pups should be wormed as soon as their eyes open, as most pups will get worms from the dam. When you see them at six to eight weeks, you should not see potbellies. It is sometimes difficult to keep growing puppies clean because they are constantly eating and producing stools. However, a concerned breeder will be diligent in cleaning up after them.

Most breeders will require a deposit from you in order to hold a pup. The balance is usually due upon taking the puppy home with you.

We highly suggest that you take a knowledgeable person with you to select a potential protection puppy. Someone usually cannot become very knowledgeable after only one day. A great amount of importance should be placed on choosing the right puppy. Remember, there is a high risk of making a mistake during this part of the process. It is wise to have someone with you who can translate the pedigrees for you and make an honest evaluation of the parents and the breeder.

THE IMPORTER

If you decide that it is an adult dog that you want rather than a puppy, you may want to utilize the services of an importer. (Do not use a broker. Brokers are those who make a living by buying quantities of dogs only for resale at some future time.) You should be aware that there are certain risks in using an importer. Again, there are specific questions you should ask to protect your investment.

1. What agencies does he import for? (If he is actively importing dogs for police departments or government agencies, then he is more likely to be on the up and up.)
2. Is there a guarantee on the dog? (How long is the guarantee good for and what is it? Money back? Replacement?)
3. Does the importer provide a complete physical, sperm count, hip check?
4. What happens if you just simply do not like the dog?

Importers usually have contacts with European kennels. They have an agent who travels to these kennels looking for *what you order*. The next step in this process is that they send you a photo and a copy of the pedigree with a price. Prices on imports can range from about $2,500 to $5,000. For example, you may be able to purchase a Schutzhund I or Ring I for approximately $3,500.

Canto Vom Heilbenbösch Sch. I. An excellent example of an imported German Shepherd Dog.

Why Use an Importer?

If you choose to go through an importer, do so with the help of a reputable trainer. This way when you get the dog, the trainer can evaluate the animal's temperament and training for you.

Dogs that come from Europe are bred carefully for strong drives and attitude. Therefore, you have a good chance of getting a very good working dog.

The service of an importer is used quite often by trainers and military and police agencies because the time necessary to train a puppy is simply too long for these people to do themselves. This is also a good way for a breeder to buy an already titled dog for breeding purposes. Many breeders have put two years of effort into a pup, only to find that the dog has a major fault or defect. This is a viable alternative to getting past those first two years of expense and work.

However, there are potential pitfalls with importers. Keep in mind that the Europeans, like Americans, do not always sell their best dogs. Many times the dogs that are sold have not met the European standards of excellence. There is always the chance of receiving a dog whose drives are not sufficient or of getting a dog that is too aggressive. While police departments need dogs with pronounced courage, a family can take a dog with a lower rating of sufficient courage.

Some of the dogs rejected from police departments can be more than adequate home protectors. *The dogs that you must avoid are the mean ones.* Police dogs do not necessarily have to be social. Remember that your home protection dog will be subjected on a daily basis to children, neighbors, other animals and the like. *A mean dog is a definite liability.*

Immediately take the animal to the vet for a thorough checkup. If there is something wrong, you will want to know about it right away. It is important that you do not get too emotionally involved until the dog is checked out.

We like to keep the dog for the owner at least for the first three days. If the dog has any type of temperament problems, we will see them during this time.

BONDING

Next the bonding process begins. We like to break bonding down into three categories:

1. The first three days, you should do nothing but spend time with the dog—petting, feeding and playing ball.
2. After this period (for the next three weeks), you will need to cover all home manners, obedience and problem-solving. Any Tracking or Agility can be worked now.
3. Following the aforementioned time periods, we work on conversion training for protection for the next three months. The dog should be bonded and finished in ninety days.

This is not to say that you will not work the dog at all in protection the first three weeks. You must check to see if your dog is workable on a training schedule, but it is best to get your dog to bond first.

WHICH IS BETTER—A PUPPY OR AN ADULT DOG?

This decision should be based solely on personal preference.

Generally speaking, if you have children or other animals, it is best to start with a puppy. The puppy will then grow up as a member of the pack and will be used to children and other animals you want the dog to live with. An adult dog may not have been raised around children, cats or horses and may behave aggressively toward them.

The adult dog usually works out best for the single person or couple without children. If there has been a recent robbery, rape or other crime the adult dog may be the only solution. On occasion, you can find trainers who have domestic-bred and trained adults for sale usually for about $2,500 to $3,000.

The advantage of buying a trained adult from a trainer is that what you see is what you get. There are no questions as to what the dog will ultimately turn out to be like. You can check health and hips at the time of purchase and know that they are unlikely to change. The dog has had the benefit of living with the trainer so conditioning is well established. You will more than likely spend less money than you would if you add up all the costs involved in raising and training a dog from the puppy stage to two years of age.

Buying an adult dog from an importer is a more complicated process. This is because you cannot be sure of the animal's background, former environment and style of training. This is very necessary to guard against people passing along "problem dogs" and making money in the process. This is a dangerous practice and the ultimate statement here is "Let the buyer beware!"

Pros and Cons of a Puppy vs. Domestic Adult or Imported Adult

Puppy

Pros:

1. Bonding period
2. Meeting sire and dam
3. Owner-involved training
4. Adjustment and socialization with children
5. Adjustment and socialization with livestock
6. Adjustment to family lifestyle

Cons:

1. Puppy problems (i.e., housebreaking, chewing, etc.)
2. May become ill and die
3. May have been stolen
4. May develop hip dysplasia or other malady
5. May not grow up with desired drives for protection
6. May grow up to be lesser breeding or show quality than desired

Domestic Adult

Pros:

1. No puppy problems to contend with
2. Fully trained, ready to go
3. Can be health-checked prior to purchase (health is not likely to change)
4. You can see the finished product (i.e., conformation and temperament)
5. Immediate protection
6. Less expensive in the long run
7. May be able to see parents or related dogs

Cons:

1. No bonding when dog was a puppy
2. May not be social with children
3. May not be social with livestock
4. May take time to adjust to your lifestyle
5. May or may not adjust to other dogs in family

Imported Adult

Pros:

1. May have strong working drives from good European stock
2. May bring in excellent lines from Europe for breeding purposes
3. Already trained and ready to go (may need conversion training for home protection purposes)
4. Can see finished product (i.e., temperament and conformation)
5. Can have immediate health check

Cons:

1. Working drives may be too strong for the family in question
2. May have been rejected in Europe due to being timid or too aggressive and, therefore, be a problem or liability
3. If there is a problem with the dog after your warranty period is up (usually two weeks), you may not have any recourse with the importer
4. Selection may be very narrow (few dogs to choose from)

The outside area is raised off the ground to help prevent disease.

*** *Warning* ***

When making the decision to purchase a dog as an adult:

This process is somewhat like buying a used car—you do not want to get home with a lemon. Every attempt should be made to check the dog over from head to tail.

There are times when a dog may appear to be all right. However, there may still be something wrong. This could be due to genetics, past experiences or a physical ailment such as a brain tumor. Although this occurs rarely, it could be fatal to the buyer if overlooked. People have been attacked, maimed and even killed by dogs with problems that were not recognized at the time of purchase.

It is imperative if you are considering buying an adult dog that you do so under the advice and supervision of a reputable veterinarian and professional trainer.

BREEDERS

During our years of experience in the dog training field, we have met many breeders. Some breed with only conformation considerations in mind. A few breed strictly with the working aspects of the dog in mind.

While it is true that both are important, common sense dictates that there must be a sense of priority here. After all, a good working dog with bad eyes, hips, knees, etc., cannot work at all. A beautiful dog without brains will be, at best, a frustrating animal to live with. A physically sound dog, with good working ability that is lacking in beauty, will be very adequate. However, to retain the Standard of the breed, we must also breed back to dogs of correct type.

In our travels, we have found that the best breeders strive to produce all three traits in one dog. Genetics being what it is, this is difficult. It is also difficult to achieve because all dogs carry recessive genes that are not always apparent until several breedings take place. This is why the true reputation of a stud dog or brood bitch is not generally apparent for a number of years. Offspring will also vary, depending greatly upon the dog or bitch the animal is bred to, as each contributes 50 percent of the genes.

One kennel located in Florida attempts to breed Rottweilers for both beauty and working ability. In order to do this, the owners have taken numerous scouting and buying trips to Germany.

We asked them why they felt this was necessary. They pointed out that in the U.S., a champion does not have to prove working ability

Money Honey Von Ironsides is an excellent specimen of a Rottweiler brood bitch. She is owned by Von Evman Rottweilers (Note her straight topline).

39

through breed suitability tests and Schutzhund titles, as they do in Germany. When breeding to an American champion, you are in no way guaranteed that the working abilities the breed is known for will be reproduced in the offspring.

After having owned American-bred Rottweilers that did not meet up to their expectations in working ability, these people set out to research the lines in Germany that were producing some of the finest working stock the country had to offer. Numerous trips were made in order to locate the right dogs and the right breeders, and they were eventually rewarded with the purchase of two fine dogs.

The dogs were sold with great reluctance on the part of their German owners and for no small amount of money. To date, Germans are still sending their bitches to be bred to these fine animals who hold multiple working and conformation titles.

Many times in the past, we have heard similar comments regarding all breeds—Rottweilers, German Shepherd Dogs, Doberman Pinschers, Belgian Malinois, etc.:

"They [fill in any country] are not going to sell us their best dogs. Typically, what we get from them is what we would consider to be 'pet quality.' In order to get the top dogs, it requires research, connections and a lot of money. The . . . consider their dogs to be livestock, so they are for sale at a price."

It should be stated that we are in no way implying that a dog not of direct European descent will not be able to handle the role of protection dog. Each dog must be judged on its own individual merits. We are dealing with odds. The odds that you will successfully train your dog through Level III protection will be greatest with a dog of European descent. They will be fifty-fifty with a purebred of unproven working background. The odds will be against you with a mixed breed (depending on the mix); however, the possibilities exist for success.

As with any endeavor, proper planning is the key. The most common mistakes are directly related to impulse buying. This is true both in the purchase of your puppy and in the selection of your training program. If you understand your goals from the outset and take the time to conduct the proper research, your chances of being disappointed with your end result will be minimized.

We are often asked why the Doberman Pinscher is not commonly used for police work in the U.S. Most people assume that the Doberman would be a logical choice as they are one of the first breeds to come to mind in connection with the term "guard dog."

We spoke with two top breeders of Doberman Pinschers, and

Aldercrest Danzig Sch. III. An excellent example of a German-style Doberman.

they point out that there are few suitable candidates to choose from in this country. With the overwhelming popularity of the Doberman in the 1970s, few breeders took working ability into consideration. Many Dobermans were bred only for beauty and therefore their working ability diminished. Today, the majority of American-bred Dobermans display weakness when exposed to stress. Sharp shyness (fear aggression) is a problem with the Doberman breed today. It is this reason, as well as health and longevity considerations, that drove these breeders to make buying trips to Germany.

They point out that in Germany, breeding stock must pass basic breeding requirements that include health and temperament tests. Breeding stock must rate very good or excellent in conformation. This process helps to weed out undesirable breeding stock.

One major difference between the European and American show Standards is that while they both judge based on the Standard, the American system allows for fads or trends. A dog in the 1970s built a certain way with considerable bone, a deep chest, etc., could do very well. However, the same type of dog in the 1990s may be considered too large and not refined enough.

A dog with a deep chest will have greater heart and lung capacity than a dog with a thin chest, and will have more stamina for the bark and hold exercises required in a working K-9. Also of consideration is the strength of the jaw. If the dog is required to carry a 4-pound dumbbell as in Schutzhund, jaw strength is required for this task.

When we asked what health problems Dobermans are susceptible to, we were told, "Although hip dysplasia is not a common problem with the Doberman, OFA Certificates ensure that the problem does not become prevalent in the future. Thyroid and heart problems are common and breeders should be questioned about this in their lines. CVI, a vertebrae problem that usually affects the neck in the Doberman and the back in German Shepherds, is a problem. It can cause paralysis in the hindquarters and result in the early death of these animals. As with severe hip dysplasia, the animal can no longer move about freely and may have to be put to sleep."

The biggest myth with regard to the Doberman as a breed is that "they turn on their masters." Any dog subjected to severe psychological or health-related problems or abuse can bite the owner. The breed of dog has nothing to do with these events.

On the whole, typical Dobermans are very family-oriented. They are quick and energetic and very willing to please. In fact, the most frequent problems with the breed stem from the dog being isolated from their families. This is definitely a breed that desires attention and they will seek it in any form possible. Negative attention is better than no attention at all. If ignored by their owners, Dobermans may bark, whine, chew or dig because of frustration, or jump on doors and gates to attract attention.

It is interesting to note that during the Doberman National Specialty put on by the Doberman Pinscher Club of America (DPCA) each year, only 25 to 30 percent of the Dobermans entered in the temperament tests pass the test. This temperament test—the Registry of Merit (ROM)—involves the dog being subjected to various stresses, such as an umbrella opening, walking over plastic sheeting, a gunshot, a person approaching, yelling, etc. It should be noted that the entries usually are made by individuals who believe their dogs have adequate balance and nerves to pass these tests. You must consider that many people do not participate because they know their dogs cannot pass these tests.

In order to produce all of the desired traits in the working breeds, many clubs have formed to promote the breeding of dogs along the lines of the German Standard. A person desiring to purchase a pup from a breeder who subscribes to this philosophy may contact the following U.S. clubs:

The ADRK is the German Rottweiler Club.

German Shepherd Dogs:	(USGDA) United States German Shepherd Dog Association
	(USA) United Schutzhund Clubs of America
Rottweilers:	(USRC) United States Rottweiler Club
Doberman Pinschers:	(UDC) United Doberman Club

CHAPTER V

Selection of the Dog or Puppy

REMEMBER, this is the most critical choice that you will make in the entire process of training a good family protection dog.

YOUR SELECTION

Unfortunately, many people put about as much effort into this decision as they would in buying a new razor or blow-dryer. Often the words "Oh he's so cute! Let's buy him!" will be uttered.

NO! NO! NO!

When you purchase what is to become the newest member of your family (and that is what the dog is!), you must be happy with the pup you will most likely live with for the next decade. This purchase will require daily attention—feeding, cleaning, grooming and training. No small effort should be expended in choosing your dog.

First you need to decide what breed will best fit into your family. For family protection, you will want to stay with your working and herding breeds as these breeds have been specifically bred for watchfulness and working ability for centuries.

It is virtually impossible to cover every breed and their pros and cons in this book. However, we will say that once you choose a breed, it is wise to thoroughly research and evaluate this breed with your own list of desired qualities.

All breeds have strengths and weaknesses. Once you have chosen your breed, seek out the best you can find. I recall that my father used to say, "It costs just as much to feed and care for an old plug as it does a thoroughbred." He was referring to horses, of course, but the same rules apply to dogs.

You should realize that when you purchase a dog for family protection, you are not looking for just any old dog—you are looking for the best. You wouldn't buy an old plug horse and then attempt to race the horse in the Kentucky Derby, would you?

When purchasing a protection dog, quality is of utmost importance. This need not be breed quality, only working quality. It is possible to find a mix that can do the job, although less likely than through a sound breeding program.

Possible breed selections follow: (These are just *some* of the candidates.)

1. Rottweiler, extra large (100–130 pounds), slower than other breeds, magnum force
2. German Shepherd Dog, large (70–100 pounds), versatile and good endurance
3. Belgian Malinois, medium (50–95 pounds), high energy, agile
4. Dutch Shepherd, medium (50–95 pounds), high energy agile
5. Belgian Sheepdog, medium (50–75 pounds), nervous, agile
6. Belgian Tervuren, medium (50–75 pounds), nervous, agile
7. Bouvier des Flandres, large (75–100 pounds), slower, lots of grooming
8. Doberman Pinscher, large (75–100 pounds), high-strung, nervous, agile
9. Boxer, medium (50–75 pounds), slower, possible breathing problems
10. Bullmastiff, large (75–100 pounds), slower and stubborn
11. Akita, large (75–100 pounds), slower, aloof, stubborn
12. Dogue de Bordeaux, extra large (80–150 pounds), slower than most, hardheaded, tenacious

As previously stated, we cannot list every possible breed. However, the breeds listed above are some of the most likely candidates.

Doberman Pinscher

Belgian Malinois

German Shepherd Dog

Rottweiler

47

LOCATING THE PROFESSIONAL BREEDER

When you are looking for the right pup, the best advice is to TAKE YOUR TIME! The biggest mistake that people make is to buy on impulse or emotion. This is easy to do when you are looking at adorable tiny furry faces. Remember that these same cute little furry faces also can grow up to have major medical or psychological problems. To avoid selecting a dog with problems such as these, it is necessary to do your homework.

The best way to find good breeders is through trainers or breed clubs. You can locate breed clubs through the AKC, dog shows, newspapers or your local dog show superintendent.

Remember that when you are looking for a dog for protection purposes, your two main concerns should be the animal's health and working ability. Beauty counts for very little. Look for parents that you can watch perform protection exercises or who have European sport titles. These help to ensure the working ability of your pup.

Research the breed you are interested in purchasing and ask what the potential health problems are. Make sure you ask if the dog's parents have been checked for these. Be sure to see the dam of the litter.

Some of the most common problems are:

Hip Dysplasia

Common in Shepherds and Rottweilers. This is a problem where the ball and socket of the hip joint do not fit together properly. Sometimes the socket is too shallow. In any case, this problem can cripple the dog or at least limit working ability. An OFA Certification on the parents is insurance, although not a guarantee against this condition. Ask to see the OFA Certificates before purchasing the pup.

Thyroid Condition

Thyroid problems are common in Rottweilers and Dobermans. Thyroid can result in obesity, reproductive problems and skin problems. This eventually will interfere with the dog's working ability.

Von Willebrand's Disease

A free-bleeding disorder, common in Dobermans, that can cause a dog to die from an otherwise nonlethal cut.

Things to check depend on where you live in the country:

- Roundworms
- Tapeworms
- Heartworms
- Whipworms
- Hookworms
- Parvovirus
- Distemper
- Hepatitis
- Leptospirosis
- Parainfluenza
- Corona Virus

Shots and worming begin in the first month of life and should be well underway by the time you purchase your puppy.

The Help of a Professional

All pups are not created equal. Whenever possible, have a professional assist you in selecting your puppy. In virtually every litter there are pups that will be better than others. It takes the trained eye of a professional to pick up on subtle differences. This is why it is a good idea to contact a trainer *before* purchasing your puppy.

What Will a Top-Quality Pup Cost?

The typical cost of a high-quality working pup will be between $500 and $1,000. Be aware that paying more does not guarantee that the dog will be better. It is possible to pay top dollar for a poor pup, so beware!

Usually the difference in cost between a $500 and a $1,000 pup will be in breeding quality. The $1,000 pup may be from more sought-after lines, and may be better suited for showing than the lower-cost pup. If you are not planning on showing or breeding, these qualities will not be as important to you.

Do Not Let Price Influence Your Decision

This is not easy to do if you are on a tight budget. However, if you invest a little bit more now, you may save money in the long run. Remember that you are in this for the long haul, and if you desire a protection dog, you are looking at two years of training this pup. All dogs do not train up equally, so if you need $200 more than you budgeted to get a good pup, wait. Save your money for the right dog. In the end, you will be glad you did.

The Best Does Not Always Cost the Most

Many people believe that paying more for something automatically means that they get more for their money. NOT TRUE! For instance, a private breeder can usually sell a pup for less because the individual does not have a lot of overhead.

PUPPY MILLS

What Is a Puppy Mill?

A puppy mill is any facility that breeds dogs for no other reason than to make money. These people are not interested in improving the breed. They do not check for disease or OFA Certificates. They do not breed with any Standard of a breed in mind.

In many cases, AKC papers are inaccurate because of sloppy record keeping, so you may not even get the pup your papers say you have. There is no AKC inspection of every litter, so the AKC has to take the word of the breeder unless there becomes a reason to question.

Many puppy mills are horrible places to see. Dogs are kept in small wire cages and are kept there in the cold or heat. They may have little or no veterinary care. They are often forced to walk and sleep in their own urine and feces. In many cases, they give birth outdoors and unattended. The mortality rate is high for puppies at birth. Overall, your chances of purchasing a puppy that will turn out to be a well-trained family protection dog are slim if the pup started out in this environment.

POUND PUPPIES

Dogs and puppies are left at the pound for a variety of reasons. Your chances of finding a good protection dog here are actually better than as described above.

Some of the reasons that dogs are in the pound are sad, unwarranted or even ridiculous—divorce, bankruptcy, death, destruction, boredom, and fear, to name a few. Some very nice dogs are left at the pound. A protection dog does not have to be a purebred.

On the other hand, many dogs in the pound are potential problems waiting to happen. A fear-aggressive dog is dangerous and will never make a good protection dog. It takes a trained eye to spot the subtle signs of a dog who looks to be a good candidate.

This is especially true since you do not get a chance to test a dog before you purchase it from the pound. This method of choosing a dog is a gamble at best. You must also realize that you could be surprised by your purchase. You may discover that your new dog is pregnant, ill or lame. Again, buyer beware!

BACKYARD BREEDERS

A backyard breeder is a person who breeds the dog(s) just for the sake of breeding. Many times they will say that they just wanted their female to have a litter. They may have a male and a female that "got together by accident." Some people say they want to let their children see pups be born.

None of these are good reasons for breeding, as these backyard breeders are not aware of things like OFA, VWD tests, worming, etc. *They are not breeding with a goal in mind*. The result, sadly, is that these pups often end up at the pound.

PROFESSIONAL BREEDERS

Professional breeders frequently do not own big fancy kennels. Some do. However, most live in a typical home or rural setting. What distinguishes this person as a professional breeder is EFFORT! The professional breeder has a definite goal in mind when breeding.

Anyone with a breeding quality female can breed her to any male desired. So why not select a stud dog who also has titles and one that offsets the faults of the female? Following are some common qualities of professional breeders:

1. Exhibit dogs in shows or trials
2. Choose top quality dogs to breed with, not just their own dog
3. Whelp puppies indoors
4. Care for the pups with quality vet care
5. Feed quality food to pups and dam

6. Screen buyers of pups
7. Sell pups with contracts
8. Will keep their pups for months if necessary to ensure they go to good homes

WHAT IF YOU PURCHASE THE WRONG PUP?

This is a very real possibility. Most people still underestimate the importance of their selection. The pup can grow up to lack the ability to be a good protection dog due to lack of temperament or to a medical or physical problem that requires the dog to live a life with a lower activity level. Abuse or mistreatment can ruin even a good dog. It is for this reason that education of the family is so important with regard to selection, raising and training of the dog.

ADULTS

One of the ways you can avoid possible disappointments when raising a pup to adulthood is to buy a young adult.

The advantage of purchasing a dog nine to twenty-four months old is that you can be more sure that the dog will have the proper temperament. You also can get the physical check for hips and health. At this stage, the dog's chances of getting a deadly disease are much less.

When you purchase an adult through a private party, trainer or importer, you should have two basic guarantees. You should be able to have the dog checked by a vet for health and hip dysplasia, and you should be able to have a trainer check the dog for training ability and temperament soundness.

This process will take four to fourteen days and a return or refund should be allowed as long as the dog is not damaged in any way. Some sellers may request to be present at these checks to ensure the safety of the animal, and you should have no problem with this. As a seller, I might also write in the agreement that if I did not feel comfortable with the owner or trainer, that I would have the option to take the dog back.

Beware of persons selling you a dog "as is" with no return policy. They are probably aware that the dog may have a problem and

A good protection prospect should not be comfortable for long when held in a submissive position.

they are trying to pass their problem on to someone else. You do not usually run into this with trainers and importers because these people should be selling with a guarantee and they should care about their ongoing reputations.

The private party, however, has nothing to lose by selling a problem dog, and may not be as educated to potential medical problems and the desired guarantees. If you want to buy a dog from a private party it would be wise to get your trainer involved to help you make the purchase.

Your puppy should be curious about noise, not frightened by it.

TRAITS TO LOOK FOR

Testing is best done by a professional, but there are certain tests and traits that you can look for.

Good protection prospects should willingly chase and play.

Prey Drive

The dog or pup should have a high Prey Drive. This means that if you drag a rag or a puppy tug in front of the dog, the pup should want to chase it and bite it (see Chapter VI, Puppy Protection Conditioning). Shaking this rag and carrying it away are all good signs.

Defensive Drive

You can note Defensive Drive by the way the pup acts in the litter. Does this pup dominate the litter, littermates or the food dish?

Does the pup bark a warning when startled by a stranger entering the room?

Noise Shyness

Take your keys and toss them *next to* your prospective puppy. A good prospect should not shy dramatically from the noise. You want to see the pup orient to the noise and then explore. If your pup takes the keys and runs away with them, this is a good sign.

Stay away from puppies who:

1. Shrink back from social contact
2. Shake with fear at noise or strangers
3. Show no willingness to chase after toys or rags
4. Scream or yelp when frightened
5. Show signs of illness

SEX: MALE OR FEMALE

(To spay or neuter, see Chapter IX.)

A common question asked with regard to protection dogs is which sex is best. Many people have preconceived notions that one or the other sex is better. Generally speaking, males have a slight edge on females as *territory* protection dogs. They are generally larger and physically stronger. They do not have the heat cycles and hormone changes every six months. They are not held up by puppies if breeding is a consideration. This is why most K-9s are male. However, we have trained females that could rival any male. As far as working ability is concerned, it has more to do with temperament than anything else. What is lacking in a dog's size and strength can be balanced with attitude and tenacity.

If the dog is going to be a house dog, then the female is usually the best choice. She is generally cleaner, smaller and more tolerant of children and strangers. The male has more problems with marking the house unless he is taught to lie down in place when he is inside. (The Place command is covered in Chapter VIII.)

As a general rule, the female has sharper instincts and will alert the household to an intruder faster than the male. The male, however, will be quicker to react with physical force. Therefore, a team of a male and female is the highest level of K-9 protection available.

The locally trained adult has some advantages over an import for the family who wants protection without an emphasis on breeding. The advantage is the knowledge of the dog's origin and training. You do not always know whether an imported dog was kept in a home or in a kennel, or was exposed to children, abused or left alone to explore during the developmental stages. This information is easily provided by the domestic trainer.

COST DIFFERENCES

The dog you choose will be with you for an average of ten to twelve years, will reside with you and your family and will become a part of your lives. This is why cost should only be one factor in your choice. It should *never* be the single determining factor of which dog you choose. And remember that it takes two years to take a puppy from eight weeks old to a fully trained protection dog.

The cost to you will add up approximately as follows:

Cost of pup	$500–$1,000
Vet care (two years)	$300–$500
	(If you're lucky)
Food and supplements (two years)	$700–$1,000
Training obedience and protection	$2,000–$3,000
	(with board)
TOTAL costs will approximate	$3,500–$5,000

(1992 general prices)

$2,500 will buy you:

- Training for your existent dog from start to finish
- An adult fully trained domestic dog
- An import who has started, but not finished training

$3,500 will buy you:

- An adult import, possibly with a title (such as Ring I, Schutzhund I or IPO I)

$4,000–$5,000 investment can bring:

- The highly trained, highly titled imports that can be used for breeding purposes as well

For the family looking for the best buy for their money, we recommend that you start from the puppy stage. If you have the time and patience, this is the best way to bond with the pup and to know everything about the dog's life experience.

Also, many imports have been raised in kennels for the purpose of becoming sport dogs or police service dogs and their preconditioning (which is very important) has been for this purpose. Therefore, if you match up a dog that has been raised for the express purpose of home protection against a kennel-raised sport or police dog, you are not going to have the same level of control, obedience or manners in the kennel-raised dogs.

For the family that does not have the time or inclination to raise a puppy, it is wise to choose a domestic trained dog. You will find that 50 percent of them will come from import lines anyway. If there is a problem with the dog, you can deal directly with the seller rather than try to deal with someone across the ocean. A good importer will back the dogs for you, but usually not for the length of time that a local seller or trainer will.

To conclude, whether you choose an adult or a puppy (domestic or import), be sure to check health and temperament guarantees prior to purchasing the animal and be sure to have a good trainer on hand to teach you how to work the dog. Remember, if you buy a pretrained adult, you still need to work with a trainer at your home so the dog understands that the dwelling is what is to be protected. It should also be emphasized that you need to be trained as well, in order to handle your dog properly.

CHAPTER VI

Raising Your Puppy— Preschool and Socialization

YOU HAVE your adorable puppy and you are now ready to embark on your training mission. There are some important things that you should take care of from the very beginning—veterinary care, nutrition, safety and general welfare.

THE THREE BASICS

Health

Have the puppy examined—an overall health check—as soon as you can. Speed is important just in case some health defect is found that will force you to return the pup. You do not want the family to become too attached to the animal in the event this should happen. It is also important to get your puppy started on a vaccination schedule that your veterinarian recommends.

Talk with your vet about diet considerations, supplements and vitamins, as different breeds require various foods and supplements. We have found that if you use top-quality chicken-and-rice or lamb-

Like a baby, your puppy has special needs.

and-rice–based dog food that ranges in the 26 to 30 percent protein range, most likely supplements won't be necessary.

Safety

Unfortunately, safety is often overlooked by many. Safety involves having all dangerous substances removed from the puppy's grasp. It also involves proper confinement so that the puppy does not get hit by a car, injured by another animal or get lost or stolen.

Puppies will chew anything. Check your home and yard for poisonous plants. Be especially aware of plants such as poinsettias, which can cause extreme illness and possible death. Remove cleaning fluids, electrical cords and small ingestible objects. The same safety concerns apply to your pup that would apply to a baby.

Confine the dog in a safe area—a dog run, puppy pen, laundry room with puppy gate, etc. This area should be free of human things.

Welfare

Welfare is the overall treatment of the puppy. Make sure your pup has the basic necessities of life—fresh food, clean water, shelter from the elements, and does not come into harm's way, whether it be an automobile, swimming pool or bad fall.

BRINGING YOUR PUPPY HOME

You want to lessen the stress of separation from the litter as much as possible. The optimum time for homecoming is seven weeks of age. The reason for this is that the pup will enter the critical fear period from eight to twelve weeks of age. If a dog becomes highly stressed during this time period, it could be detrimental to overall sound development.

Bring the puppy home early in the day if possible, to allow adjustment to new surroundings before being left alone at night to sleep. Try to get the same food the breeder uses, and have it on hand. Do not change the diet right away. The dog will be under enough stress with the change in environment. You do not want to create another stress at the same time. A puppy's intestinal system is delicate and takes time to get used to a new food. If you do choose to change foods, do it at least three weeks later and at 25 percent intervals.

Like a baby's playpen, an exercise pen is safe and portable.

PUPPY PENS

A puppy pen can be bought or made. It is a playpen area that should be at least 5 feet by 8 feet, if not larger. The floor area should be temporarily covered with newspapers. The pup should have a crate at one end with a comfortable blanket inside. Food and water should be kept close to the sleeping area as you want to encourage elimination away from the sleeping area.

The new puppy should be kept indoors free from drafts, flies and other animals. The puppy pen can be set up inside the house or garage. If you choose the garage, make sure that during daylight hours the lights are on. Also be sure the room is kept at a reasonable temperature and air circulation is adequate.

Some people choose to keep their pups in a gated laundry room, bathroom or kitchen. This is fine, temporarily. After a while you are also risking destruction of the area.

Protection breeds are generally large and therefore they create large messes. This is why the puppy pen is the best choice. Remember, the puppy will not be fully vaccinated until he is four months old. For this reason, you will want to prevent exposure to diseases as much as possible while your pup is growing. Your primary concerns from the age of seven weeks to four months are as follows:

1. Keep the new arrival clean and safe.
2. Do not go to public places such as parks, school grounds, kennels or puppy training classes until your pup reaches four months of age. Coming into contact with other dogs (or places they may have eliminated) may expose your puppy to diseases.
3. Give safe things to chew on and keep unsafe things out of reach.
4. Gradually introduce things that will be a part of the pup's life on a regular basis (i.e., birds, children, livestock, etc.). Do not wait as this exposure will be harder later on. Protect your pup from harm while doing this.
5. Have the trainer come to your home to show you how you can work with the pup at this age. Your sessions will be short—approximately ten minutes at a time—as the attention span is minimal at this age. Everything should be positive.

CONFINEMENT CONDITIONING

One of the most important concepts in this book is confinement conditioning. If used properly, this concept will allow you to do two things successfully:

1. Raise a puppy that by one year of age will be totally trustworthy both in the house and yard.
2. Protect your personal belongings and your yard from any and all destruction due to improper behavior on the puppy's part.

To comprehend and apply this concept, you must first have an open mind and be willing to understand life from your dog's point of view. The following are some basic elements of dog psychology that you should be familiar with:

1. The dog does not have the ability to reason. This means he or she cannot comprehend that chewing your new leather shoes is BAD. The value placed on items is a human concept. The dog doesn't know the difference between chewing on your Gucci shoes, a stick or a bone. The good news is that the dog can be taught by association not to chew on your things; however, the way you go about this teaching process will be the important factor.
2. Dogs do not understand spanking as punishment. Spanking or hitting the animal serves only one purpose—to teach the dog to fear you and to be submissive. Both are undesirable traits in a protection dog. DO NOT STRIKE YOUR PUP!
3. Dogs learn correction through trial and error. If they try something and the action results in pleasure or a reward, they will be likely to repeat the same action again. In some cases, the act will become a conditioned response because it has been repeated so many times that it becomes habit. In the case of a negative association with an action, the action is not likely to be repeated. If it is repeated and the same negative association is provided again, the dog will be less likely to attempt the same action. Eventually, it will become a conditioned behavior to avoid the undesirable behavior.
4. The only glitch to this conditioning process is the chance that the outcome of a behavior will be inconsistent. If this happens, true conditioning cannot take place. In the dog's mind, he has had a chance at getting a positive response for an action, so

it is worth trying. That is why it is imperative that you be able to completely control the outcome of your dog's actions.

5. You may say, "But I know that my dog understands what she has done wrong. When I come home and she has done something wrong she cowers. When she has behaved well she greets me happily."

The explanation for this is what is referred to as "chaining" or "sequencing." This refers to the dog's ability to understand that a certain sequence of events will lead to an action. This is a conditioned response (i.e., owner leaves, dog destroys, owner returns, owner yells and spanks the dog, the animal then cowers). After a certain amount of conditioning, the dog will cower because she understands the routine. Leave out one element of the chain of sequencing, and the dog will not cower. This does not, however, have any relation to understanding that the action was **wrong**.

You must remember that right and wrong are human concepts. They are not concepts in the animal kingdom. Dogs work primarily from instinct and conditioning. They possess intelligence, it is just a different type of intelligence than ours.

What Is Confinement Conditioning?

This is the action of confining the pup when we cannot actively condition his behavior. To do this, we recommend a puppy pen when he is little, an airline shipping crate and a dog run as he gets older.

Avoid the Cage Complex

The typical human reaction to the concept of using a crate is "I don't want to keep my dog in a cage." There are several reasons for us to think this way. We feel guilty about animals we see at the zoo and our natural inclination is to humanize dogs.

The truth of the matter is that confinement is not cruel unless it is excessive. Confinement is used for three reasons—the dog's safety, the safety of your possessions and as a training aid to ultimately allow for your dog's freedom. What good is freedom to your dog if it creates injury or havoc within your household? The best course of action is to give freedom in small doses and teach the dog how to behave with it.

Dog Run

A dog run (5 feet by 20 feet or longer for a larger dog) provides safety from harm in a chain link area. In this area, your dog should have a bucket of fresh clean water, a clean dog house and should be fed out of stainless steel bowls that should be thoroughly cleaned after each feeding. The base should be cement (the cleanest) or gravel rock. This area can double as the dog's bedroom.

Airline Crate (Fiberglass)

This is used as a bed for the dog to sleep indoors or out, away from the elements and without disturbing your home. This helps to condition the pup that when in the house, there is one spot that can be a kind of home base.

If this is seen as a bed and place of comfort, your pup will accept it and seek it out. Dogs are den-oriented creatures and often seek out a dark corner behind a chair or find solitude under a desk or table.

The advantages (for both you and your dog) in using a fiberglass crate follow:

- For safety when you transport the dog whether in a truck, van or via airplane.

This puppy kennel is on a platform with rollers for easy cleaning.

- When taking your dog on a trip where you will stay in a hotel, tent or other unfamiliar place. It will allow you to safely leave the dog for a couple of hours while you hike, eat out, fish, etc.
- Allows you to keep your dog safely while in close proximity to other dogs. Fiberglass crates are required at many training kennels and clubs. They also come in handy at dog shows and special events.
- Using a crate in the house will allow you to keep any dirt and hair in one place for easier cleanup.

Start using the crate in the puppy pen when the pup is seven weeks to four months of age. On bright sunny days, the puppy can go out in a dog run without a problem as long as flies are not present. At four months of age bring the pup into the house in the fiberglass crate. Your pup can remain in the run during the day.

SOCIALIZATION USING THE CRATE

The crate can be used as an aid in socialization. It provides a safe place for the pup to view and smell the world with safety. The dog can become familiar with sights, sounds and smells without stress. After this initial warm-up, you can then (with close supervision) bring the puppy out for a closer view or physical contact with the subject of the socialization process.

CONDITIONING USING CONFINEMENT

The conditioning portion of confinement conditioning is the key. Confinement itself is not a solution or a way to keep the dog for life. It begins as a necessity and should end up as a convenience. Confinement by itself will create undesirable behaviors in a dog such as demanding time and attention by acting up. Barking or self-mutilation can be a result of a neglected dog who is left alone. This is not the idea of crate training.

Conditioning is the process whereby you set out to teach the animal what is acceptable behavior when out in the yard or home. Conditioning must be supervised; therefore, it is up to the owner how much time he or she spends each day on the conditioning process. The rule of thumb is the dog should definitely not be crated more than twelve hours of a twenty-four-hour day. Typically, eight hours are

Use of a Fiberglas crate protects baby and puppy from each other.

sleeping hours. In families, the other four hours will most likely be used on and off while the family is in the house eating, watching TV or engaged in similar activities.

In the House

The pup may be brought out at any time when directly supervised by someone. Be particularly careful when the dog is on carpeting. If the pup has an accident on the carpet, you will have two problems on your hands:

1. If the urine goes through to the pad, you will not be able to clean it 100 percent.
2. Because you cannot clean it 100 percent, the pup will be twice as likely to return to the spot and do it again.

If the pup is not lying with you quietly, a good idea is to use a baby gate with the dog on a tile or linoleum floor. In case of an accident, the area can be totally cleaned. Avoid accidents at all costs because you do not want to start a conditioning process of the puppy urinating and defecating in the house. Take the pup out frequently and most definitely after all feedings and naps.

In the Yard

The puppy may be brought out of the pen to run or to play in the yard under supervision. This will allow you to stop or correct any improper action on the spot. All interaction between children and the pup should be watched carefully to protect both from each other. At times, even the best behaved children can be mean or overwhelming with puppies.

On-the-Spot Corrections

The whole premise of confinement conditioning is your ability to make on-the-spot corrections when problems occur. Just how to make these corrections is covered in the chapter on problem-solving.

If left alone in your house and yard, a young dog is very likely to become destructive. If you are not there to correct, your pup may learn that this behavior is rewarding and you will have started a negative conditioning cycle. After the fact, there is nothing to be gained by punishing the dog. As we stated before, unless the animal is caught in the act, there will be no association of action with the reprimand.

The End Result of Confinement Conditioning

Confinement conditioning is the most humane way to train your puppy—you do not have to use physical corrections or "stress out" or cause the animal to fear you. Confinement is not cruel. It ensures the safety and security of the dog while ensuring the safety of your property. Your dog should only be confined as much as *you* want or allow. The process of confinement puts you in control and, therefore, it can only be misused or abused if you allow it to be. The end result after approximately one year of conditioning is that the dog has learned how to live in the house and in the yard, and can spend all of the time in the house and yard with total freedom if you like.

Some people choose to continue to use kennels or crates on a part-time basis—when hosting parties, when their children are playing in the yard or when workers are coming in and out of the home. This is wise with a protection dog. You want your dog to be social; however, you do not want to "oversocialize."

PUPPY PRESCHOOL

Puppy owners are also confused about when they should start training the pup. They have heard answers ranging from four months to one year. The multitude of various opinions can be confusing.

The truth is that you begin training as soon as the puppy adjusts to your home, but on a level the pup can handle. Do not expect from an eight-week-old puppy what you would expect from a four-month-old dog. Do not expect from a four-month-old what you would expect from a six-month-old. Also, just because your eight-month-old may look like an adult, do not expect adult behavior.

As with children, every age has its stages. For most breeds, maturity sets in when the animal reaches two years of age, although with some large breeds (i.e., Giant Schnauzers) do not expect maturity to set in until age three. In reality, everything you do will teach your puppy something. This is why you need to establish a system from the very start.

Starting Your Puppy

Your attitude should always be to BE POSITIVE and to NOT STRESS THE PUPPY! There will be lots of time to teach what your pup needs to know. Right now you want to give a positive impression of the relationship with the handler. This is not really Obedience training, but rather preconditioning for Obedience.

For this purpose, we will use food to motivate the puppy. When food is used properly, you will eliminate all stress. The four commands you will want to start with are: Heel, Sit, Come and Down. You may do this in any language as long as you are consistent. Choose a time when the pup is hungry and use food not normally given (i.e., pieces of hot dogs, chicken or liver).

The stationary commands are the easiest. Warm up the puppy by starting with these first. It is recommended that you do this inside the house where there are generally fewer distractions.

Sit

Hold a tidbit of food in front of the puppy's nose and raise it slightly above the head so the pup has to bend back to look up at it. Command "Sit" in a calm voice. The dog's rear end should naturally go down if you hold the food in the right position. As soon as your pup sits, praise with "Good Sit" and give the treat. *Remember, always*

Sit—Let the food guide the puppy into the sitting position.

Puppy Down—The leash is held firmly as the puppy is directed down with use of food.

be positive and offer lots of praise. Do not get frustrated and do not start pushing the pup. There is no hurry. If you do start to get frustrated, try again later or another day.

Down

Hold a tidbit in front of the puppy's nose and lower it to the ground and a little forward, letting the dog follow the food. Command "Down." The dog's rear end may stay up in the air. If this happens, gently push the rear down as long as the front end is down. If the front end pops up, start all over again. Once the whole dog is down, say "Good Down." Keep the tidbit low, give it and stroke the dog gently along the back. Repeat "Good Down." Allow the dog to get right back up again if desired. Do not fight to keep your dog down.

Leash Training

For the next two commands you will need a leash and a collar. Before you begin, make sure the puppy is used to the leash and collar. They should be flat, either nylon or leather. The puppy can wear the collar constantly. The leash should only be used when you are present. Do not allow chewing on the leash—distract the pup with something else.

Walking on Leash (Heel)

Teaching the puppy to walk on a leash requires a fairly large area to work. Walking in a circle is confusing. You want to downplay use of the leash so the puppy does not panic and pull away.

In order to do this, hold the leash loosely and hold the tidbit in front of your pup's nose. Command "Heel" and make the dog follow the food. Since the Heel command is carried out on the left, start with the pup on your left. While walking, praise with "Good Heel." Walk slowly and stop often. Use the same technique shown earlier for Sit. Have the dog sit at your left side and reward with praise and the tidbit.

Come

Now that the pup is fully aware that you hold the tidbit, move back and away. Call the dog by *name* and say, "Buck, Come." Hold out the treat and show it. Draw Buck in and ask him to sit in front of you. Use the sit technique the same as you did previously. Praise as

Heel—With use of food reward, the puppy will hardly know she's on the leash.

Come—Direct the food to the puppy's level.

before, "Good Come, good Sit," and reward with the food. Do this for *short* periods of time. Stop if you see the dog becoming bored, tired and/or distracted. Remember that the main goal is to keep it fun and positive.

Other things to teach your pup on a very positive level using food or a toy reward follow:

1. Fetch—throw a toy a short distance, command "Bring."
2. Jump—small objects 4–6 inches high, command "Hup."
3. Find it—search for a toy or person, command "Find."
4. Stay—use stay for very short periods and then release the dog by saying "Okay." Stay is hard for young pups because of their short attention spans.

PUPPY PROTECTION CONDITIONING

1. Use a puppy tug. Tie a leash to one end and drag it and allow the puppy to chase it, bite it and hold it. Give some resistance and then reward by letting him carry away the tug. With a very young pup you may use a burlap sack instead.
2. Let the puppy bite at the tug. Play a short game of tug-of-war and let the pup win. Let your dog carry the tug away.
3. Have someone hold the pup on a leash, stand in one place and let the pup have all of the six-foot leash. Approach and tease the pup with the tug, moving it side to side. As the pup reaches out to grab the tug, hold it so that it sets in the back of the jaws. This will help him to learn to bite deep where his power is. Reward with a quick game of tug and let him have it.
4. Next, using this same technique, start to pet and stroke as the pup bites, while you keep tension on the tug. Then release and let your dog have the tug.
5. The last step is to teach Buck to hang on while his head is turned from side to side. Do not turn it too far. The idea is to teach him to use his mouth in every possible position.

Things you should know about puppy conditioning:

1. *Always carry out these steps under the supervision of a licensed professional trainer.* There are many ways you can make mistakes that could permanently damage or ruin your pup.

2. Always use a puppy tug for this process. Do not use towels, clothing, etc. This will only form bad habits both in the pup's biting capacity and in "stealing" things in the home.
3. Do not let the puppy bite on your arms and hands in play. This actually encourages soft biting which is nonproductive and can cause minor injuries to children and others. At the very least, it can become irritating.
4. The tug is meant as a teaching tool only. It is not to be left for the dog to play with alone. Store it in a safe place when it is not being used.
5. *Put the tug away when the pup starts teething at approximately four months of age*. Do not use it at this time as it could hurt the puppy's mouth. Wait until all puppy teeth are out to begin using it again.

Confinement conditioning will help to minimize the stress of raising the puppy. Even so, you will run into problems such as housebreaking, chewing, digging, playful biting, jumping on people and stealing things. To deal with these, refer to the next chapter.

Puppies derive pleasure from destroying plants.

A negative association with this act will discourage such behavior.

CHAPTER VII

Problem-Solving

THE MOST COMMON reason that people call a dog trainer is for problem-solving. Using K-9 Companions' system of confinement conditioning (see Chapter VI), along with our system of instinctual corrections, you should be able to prevent problems before they start.

HOUSEBREAKING

Housebreaking begins as soon as you purchase your puppy. The most effective way to go about housebreaking is prevention. You must adhere to a routine for elimination that the puppy can count on. As a rule of thumb, the pup should be put out every two hours, after each meal and after waking (in the morning or following naps). The puppy should be monitored carefully when not in a crate.

Newspaper on the floor should only be used as a temporary measure when the pup has to be left in the pen while you are away. The dog should not be left in the house at this time as this can result in confusion as to why it is okay to go to the bathroom in the house at one time, but not at another. A garage pen is preferable. However, this may not be possible if you live in an apartment complex.

Doggy Door Method

Most people with large pups prefer not to use a doggy door. However, if this is the method you choose, you must anticipate some inconvenience while the dog is being conditioned to use the door.

This method should be taught step-by-step. Start with pushing the crate up to the flap of the doggy door at convenient times during the day. That way the pup can only come into the house and *enter* the crate and can only go out into the yard by exiting *from* the crate. This takes away the ability to eliminate in the house. Always supervise the pup in the yard when you are at home unless you have the ability to access the doggy door to a dog run—an ideal arrangement.

As the puppy becomes conditioned to go out the doggy door to eliminate (a one to three week process), try moving the crate back and block off a small area just large enough to allow space to lie outside the crate. This gives a little more space. As long as the pup hits the door to eliminate, keep this space. One to three weeks later, give more space until the dog gradually has the entire room. Be especially careful with carpeted areas, as dogs will generally seek the most absorbent surface to eliminate on. Inexpensive carpet runners can be purchased to solve this potential problem.

Open each additional room or space to the puppy *slowly* and with close supervision. If you hurry this process, you increase the likelihood of making a mistake.

It is imperative that you do not try these methods without strictly supervising the puppy. Allowing the pup too much freedom of movement, without close supervision, is unwise. Leaving a dog unsupervised will also result in mistakes and destruction that will ultimately be counterproductive to your conditioning. Keep in mind that you are conditioning with the goal of trusting the dog at one year of age.

Crate Training Method

This is the preferred method for large dogs simply because of their size. We prefer to teach the pup to come in and lie down in one spot. This will keep the dog out of the way when you want to eat, watch television or entertain.

To begin this method, the dog must be between eight and sixteen weeks old. Bring the puppy in—using the crate for two hours at a time—and then take your dog out to "exercise." The pup should only be out of the crate in the house when with you.

At four months of age, the pup will have a more precise form of

Obedience training. At this time, allow your dog to lie down in the Place outside of the crate when you are present. Since the pup is not allowed to roam freely in the house without you, there will be no temptation to eliminate in the house.

Corrections in Housebreaking

Confinement conditioning eliminates 90 percent of your need to make a correction. Mistakes will sometimes occur, usually due to owner error. When they happen, you need to show the pup you are not pleased. REMEMBER, above all else, to **KEEP YOUR COOL!**

If you happen to witness a mistake, your immediate objective should be to startle the dog. Yell a sharp "NO," put the pup's nose down *next to* the mess, *but not in it*. Shake the dog firmly by the scruff of the neck (this is what "mother" would do) and go to where you wanted your dog to eliminate to begin with.

Carry the stool or soaked-up urine in a paper towel and put it down where you want the dog to go. Show the spot and praise the dog. Allow time for elimination in the proper area. Return to the soiled area and clean it the best you can with one of the several products on the market (sold at pet stores) to aid cleanup and mask odors. Remember that if this happens using our methods, it is because of your failure to supervise. Do not allow the puppy to return to this area in the near future. If the dog eliminates in the right area, praise and reward with a tidbit.

CHEWING

All puppies relish chewing as it is natural to the teething process. You must provide safe things for your pup to chew on—English rubber toys, nylon bones, cow hooves and rawhide. Avoid rawhide with knotted ends as it can be swallowed in large chunks and caught in the dog's throat and intestines. Anything that can be ingested carries a risk. Unfortunately, these are the playthings that dogs desire the most. Large shank bones or knucklebones from the butcher are the safest natural bones. Boil them and remove all of the excess fat. Throw away these bones every three to four days to avoid bacteria, ants and dirt. Supervise your pup as much as possible. If you cannot be there to supervise, it is best to leave the pup with the safest of toys.

If you find that your pup is chewing on something undesirable, the least stressful correction that the dog will understand is to immediately replace the improper object with a safe toy. You will find, however, that good potential protection puppies have very strong wills and often will defy your attempts to deter them. This calls for a correction, as it is important for the pup to know that you are always in charge.

Chewing Corrections

As mentioned previously, the dog perceives the world through the five senses. Therefore, it is best to use instinctual corrections that your pup can understand, instead of physical corrections.

Instinctual Correction

Instinctual corrections should be used to deter, distract or startle the pup. Depending upon the strength of the pup's nervous system, you will find some of these corrections will work better than others.

The senses we are working on follow:

- Hearing (sound that startles or distracts; i.e., a shake can, a rock thrown against wood, etc.)
- Taste and smell (a negative association with an object due to bad taste or smell)
- Touch (primarily water to startle or distract). In extreme life-threatening cases, such as poison food, mild shock using poison-proofing device. *Shock collars cause neuroses*, as the dog is unable to get away from the source of the shock. Typically they are a shortcut or a quick fix to a problem that can be taken care of through long-term conditioning.

Glop for Problem Chewers

Recipe for "Glop"—a hot, soapy mixture:

In a cup, mix two parts liquid dish soap with one part pepper (preferably cayenne or red pepper rather than black pepper, or you can mix all three.)

You can apply Glop to any problem spots in the yard, such as telephone or cable wires, wood surfaces, etc. *Caution: Do not* apply this mixture to open wounds on plants as it might irritate or kill them.

The dog will most likely investigate and find out that these spots no longer taste or smell good. You can use Glop as a prevention method to keep the dog from chewing objects to begin with.

Problem Articles

If the pup is constantly after a certain pair of shoes or a baby toy, leave the article out and watch the pup go for it. The first thing you do is to startle with a shake can. Shake cans are made from aluminum soft drink or beer cans. A half dozen pennies are put inside the can. Toss the shake can *toward* the pup (*never at* the dog) and yell a firm "NO!"

Go to the dog, do not call the dog. Put the Glop on the article and put the dog's nose up to it to get some of the offensive mixture on the dog's mouth. Say "NO" and release. Give a toy and say "Good dog." Leave the offending article where it was so that the pup can return to investigate, only to discover that this is the source of the bad taste and smell. If you repeat this process regularly with any object, you will find that the dog will not repeat the mistake after one or two attempts. CAUTION: Wash all baby toys after doing this so that your children do not get Glop in their eyes or mouths.

NOTE: With *all* corrections, it is important to *show* the pup the *desired* action or toy. Next, praise and return the dog's spirit to a balanced level.

PLAYFUL BITING/JUMPING

The shake can's primary use is to startle the dog. It should *never* be left with the dog as a toy or it will lose its effectiveness. Keep the shake cans in strategic places such as near doors or gates where children come into contact with the dog.

Hold the can behind your back and out of sight. When your dog jumps or bites, vigorously shake the can near the pup's face holding it by the top for maximum volume sound. Sternly say "No!" When the pup stops, even if only for a second, put the can behind your back and praise. Distract with something else positive, such as a toy, or use a tidbit and say "Sit," then praise.

It is important to realize that all pups seek attention or play. You can satisfy these needs; however, you want to positively mold methods of seeking this attention. *Never let children under ten years of age use the shake can.* Children tend to think it is a game to scare the pups. *Do not allow this method to be abused.* You only want to startle not scare the dog. After the correction, it is vital that you build the dog's spirit back up with praise.

An untrained dog.   A trained dog.

Outside you can use a water correction for jumping and play biting. Get yourself a large glass of cold water. If the pup runs to attack your pant leg, simply dump the water on the dog while saying "No!" When the dog backs away, praise. Give the command "Sit" and give attention. Change the subject, pick up a toy and throw it. *It is always desirable to make a quick correction and follow it up with praise.*

DIGGING

Digging should be almost nonexistent due to confinement conditioning. Again, correction by prevention will stop the problem from happening to begin with. You will need a method of correction if you look up and see the pup digging. On-the-spot correction is important so the dog can make the association.

First, startle by tossing your shake can and yelling "No!" If you do not have a shake can, look for another way to startle *without physically hurting the dog*. Throw a rock (or any object that will make a noise) at a nearby wooden fence or trash can. Use a hose or anything to startle. When the dog stops the undesirable action, give a toy and praise.

Next, you will want to create a negative association with the digging spot. Two possible ways of doing this follow:

1. Take some of the dog's stool and put it in the hole. Cover it only slightly with dirt so that the pup will be repulsed.
2. Take some Glop and dump it in the hole so that the dog will be repulsed.

EXCESSIVE BARKING OR WHINING

Many times a pup will try to gain attention by barking or whining. It is very important that you learn to read this communication. Your puppy will send out different types of barks or whines that will have different meanings, i.e., hunger, pain, boredom, defensiveness, fear, discomfort, attention-getting, frustration, excitement and so on. You should never correct for communicating with you unless it is unwarranted and/or excessive.

Corrections

As we have previously discussed, first you must know what is being communicated to you. If your dog is just "talking" for no particular reason or rebelling to be let in or out, and this is not what you desire, two options for correction follow:

1. Make the dog more comfortable by providing music, toys or safe things to chew on, or cover the crate with a sheet so your pup can sleep.
2. Correct by squirting water, shaking the shake can or throwing a rock against a wooden fence to make noise near the crate. Always say "No!" in conjunction with this. *Resist rewarding this behavior by letting the dog out or giving attention.*

We must stress that the most important point in this section of the book is that you **DO NOT HIT YOUR DOG!** If you notice any of the instinctual corrections mentioned here result in anything more than startling or deterring the dog, discontinue use and consult your trainer. *As with everything else in this system, it should be handled under the supervision of a licensed trainer.*

Every dog has an individual temperament and nervous system. A good protection prospect should possess a strong-enough temperament and nervous system that none of these nonphysical corrections should have adverse impact. If they do, it is questionable whether the pup will turn out to have strong enough nerves to be a protection dog.

Remember that the elimination of puppy problems requires patience and consistency. Do not allow yourself to become stressed during this process as it will all work out in the long run.

CHAPTER VIII

Home Manners

HOME MANNERS are defined as the limits that you set for the puppy in your home environment. There are three standard home manners:

Boundary Control: Teaching the pup to stay within set boundary limits in the house or in the yard. Teaching the pup not to go into the street unless you say it is "OKAY." These are safety rules.

Door Crashing: Another safety rule is teaching the pup not to go in or out of doors or gates unless you say it is "OKAY."

Place Command: Teaching the pup to come into the house and lie down in a specific place in the house. There are typically one to three places that are "his" or "hers" in the house. This command will work well for your protection later.

HOME MANNERS TRAINING AT
FOUR MONTHS OF AGE

Boundary Control

First you need to decide where you want your boundaries to be. In most homes, we recommend starting with curbs leading into the street. Next, we move to the sidewalk boundaries leading to the neighbors' yards. Many times these boundaries are not clearly marked. Temporarily use a garden hose or a board across this area until the dog is conditioned. Some people would rather have the dog stop at the sidewalk (or in the case of a condominium complex, the boundary may be at a garage door).

This is a simple procedure. First, walk the pup along the boundary that you have chosen. Use a 6-foot leash and a standard choke/slip-type training collar. Bring the dog to the curb and slowly step into the street. If the pup attempts to follow you, give a quick jerk-and-release on the collar and say ''No!'' Praise as the dog backs up.

You must correct quickly when the dog steps into the street. Your ''No'' must project the urgency you would feel if the pup were about to be struck by a car. Praise must be sincere and exuberant when your dog returns to the curb.

Teaching your dog not to leave her boundaries could save her life.

After you practice on curbs for several days, proceed to sidewalk boundaries. These boundaries are less obvious. It will be necessary to place something across the sidewalk so that the pup will easily notice it. Practice stopping at this point.

The Release Word: "Okay"

Now that your dog stops at the correct boundaries, what if you want to go for a walk and your pup refuses to leave the yard? Now you can teach the release word—"Okay." Do not overdo this as you do not want to undo the conditioning that you have started. You will want to do this in conjunction with Obedience training so that you can say, "Okay, Buck, Heel." This way, the dog understands that this is Obedience when you allow a release. It is not a release which allows the dog to run down the street.

When you give the "Okay," gently pull the pup toward you and praise. Command "Heel" and walk off with Buck in the Heel position at your left side. Heel is explained more fully in Chapter X. Praise as you walk and keep your pup's spirit up.

The next step in boundary work is to add distance and distractions. Advance to a 30-foot-long line. Let it drag on the ground as you walk the dog toward the street. Never use a command when you are working boundary control, except after you have released with an "Okay." Talk to your pup as you might when you are relaxed. "Buck, want to play?" or "Let's go." If Buck forgets and walks into the street, quickly turn and say "No!" If you need to, pick up the long line and use it to correct. Do this several times in different areas of the boundary.

Next, bring out a ball or a toy. Bounce it in the street. Have children tempt your dog, try food—anything the dog could possibly encounter. Be consistent with your corrections. Do this on a regular basis until the dog is six months old and you could be ready to finish the process off leash.

BOUNDARY TRAINING—SIX MONTHS

Using only a short leash (See "Tab" in Chapter X), review the same procedure you have been practicing for the last eight weeks. First, try this with the dog next to you, then gradually add distractions and distance. Know how trustworthy your dog is. Use extreme caution if you live on a busy street.

DOOR CRASHING

The term "door crashing" can be misleading. Door crashing involves teaching the dog not to crash *out of or into* doors or gates. We handle this in almost the same way as boundary control except for the fact that door crashing is taught both in and out.

There are many reasons for this. The two most common are:

1. To keep the dog from escaping from the house or yard
2. To keep the dog from knocking you over as you go in or out of your doors or gates

Again, this is not difficult to do, but requires consistency and repetition. Bring the pup to the doorway on the leash. Walk through, but correct if the pup tries to walk through. Give a quick jerk backward with a firm "No!" Praise while the dog stays there. It is this simple to show what you want. Talk, but do not let your pup come to you until you say the magic word—"Okay." Once you release, you can praise and pet the dog. Next, turn around and do the same thing coming the other way.

After you have the pup conditioned to wait until you (and anyone else) walk through the door before you release, you can begin something more difficult. Use distractions such as strangers to try to cause a mistake. The pup quickly will learn not to be tricked and to make the proper choice to follow what the handler has asked.

Position should be maintained behind the door or gate, regardless of the temptations of food, children, toys, cats and so on.

Six Months—Door Crashing

After practicing for eight weeks, you should be able to enforce the same rules using *only* the tab. The pup should now be able to go from place to place *in the house and yard* without a leash.

PLACE COMMAND

The place command provides the following benefits to you and your dog:

1. Allows you and your dog to spend more time together. The dog can be with you even when you are doing daily chores you might otherwise do alone.

A well-trained dog will properly greet you at the door.

2. Allows 90 percent of dog hair and dirt to be in one location for quick and easy cleanup.
3. Allows the family to compromise if one family member doesn't want the dog in the house and others do. The dog's place can be just inside a door on a tile entry surface.
4. *The dog can only protect you when with you. This command will maximize the time you can spend together.*
5. If you own your own business, the place command can also be used there. Many people take their dogs to work with them daily for personal protection.

Place Command at Four Months

Your pup should be used to coming into the house in the crate by now. It should not be any great shock to enter the house.

To effectively teach the Place command, the pup must already understand basic Obedience. It is essential for the dog to comprehend the Down and Stay commands to master the Place command.

Bring the pup in the house on a leash. As you release through the doorway, begin to command Place, leading the dog to the spot you have chosen. When you get to this spot, point down as in the Down command. Use the same correction and praise system as taught in Obedience in Chapter X. Praise with "Good Place!" The first few times you may say "Stay"; however, this practice should be halted quickly.

Start with the dog in place for ten to fifteen minutes and work up to two hours at a time. Of course, if your dog stays quiet or falls asleep, leave well enough alone. If the dog is playing "jack-in-the-box" with you and jumps up every time you turn your back, you will need to work in small doses. The rule of thumb is the dog gets one mistake and correction. If there is a second mistake, put the dog in a place where you are out of sight for ten to fifteen minutes before you try again. This will teach that if your dog wants to be with you, he or she must do as you wish.

You will generally have a tougher time teaching the Place command to more active breeds (i.e., Shepherds and Dobermans) than you will have with the larger, slower types such as Rottweilers and Bullmastiffs. In any case, you must be patient and stay the course. Remember that you are working for the end result.

At four months, you should always use the leash for the Place command, preferably a nylon leash as the pup will be less likely to chew on nylon than on leather.

An open crate allows a dog to Place and still protect.

Six Months—Place Command

At six months, you should have practiced eight weeks of conditioning using the leash.

After you have practiced your basic five Obedience commands off leash, you are ready to do Place without the leash. Use a tab so that you can correct if and when you need to.

Now when you two go through the door, tell your pup to Place without going there also. If you need to go part of the way, point to the spot. Your ultimate goal is to get the dog to go to Place automatically and alone. Once there, the dog should remain unless released.

You can help the dog enjoy a place by making it comfortable. If it is on the tile, make it warm in the winter by using a blanket, rug or bed. During the summer months, the tile is cool. Give something safe to chew on and from time to time, also give a treat. This way, your dog will find satisfaction without moving from the spot. It is also wise to periodically verbally praise. Give the pup physical attention so there is no necessity to get up to seek attention.

Suggestions for Place

Keep your dog out of the path of travel. The place should *not* be between the television and the refrigerator where people will constantly be stepping over the dog. Instead, designate a place where your dog can see you, will not try to move in order to see you and will be out of the way.

Ideal places include:

- Entry areas by the front door
- A corner of the kitchen or family room
- An unused fireplace or hearth
- Under a high table
- Next to dad's favorite chair
- Next to the bed (not on it!)

Never let your dog sit or lie on your couch or bed with you. This will elevate your dog in the pack order (a dog's way of thinking of your family). Often, this will result in unwanted characteristics such as possessiveness, usually of the dominant opposite sex member in the household, possessiveness of that piece of furniture, and stubbornness and willfulness toward members of the family the dog feels are subordinant.

If adhered to on a regular basis, home manners will help to keep the dog subordinant, but not submissive, within the family and will squelch the tendency for stubborn and willful behavior that can be a problem with the kind of temperament a protection dog must have.

CHAPTER IX

You and Your Dog—Setting Goals

UNTIL NOW, all of your training has been short-term and positive. You have not expected precision of any sort. It is time to raise your expectations just a bit. The attention span has grown and the dog is out of the critical fear period.

Begin to correct your dog for being slow (or for refusing) to respond. Teach the Stay command and expect a Stay of three to ten minutes or longer if the dog is down. Maximum Sit/Stay should be three minutes at this age. Once a dog reaches this age, we drop 90 percent of the food reward and rely almost solely on praise.

READING YOUR DOG

The type of training collar that you use, as well as the strength of your correction, will be based on the dog's temperament.

While training your dog, you will be part of a balancing act. This is in reference to the delicate balance of correction and positive motivation. This balance is very important because you must give a stern enough correction to let the dog know that you are in control. At the same time, you do not want to correct so severely that you bring down your dog's confidence level.

The dog and handler should form a cohesive team.

An excellent example of dog and handler synergy.

Some pups will be very sensitive and a slight correction with a raised voice will be all that is needed. Others will pay little or no attention to this type of correction and will require a very stern correction to pay attention.

A good trainer will be able to quickly discern the pup's temperament and advise you how to proceed. Because you are looking for protection from this pup, you are best off if this is the tough guy who requires a little harder correction. This type of pup is a bit more difficult to deal with during the first year of life because of being so assertive. However, this will be a better dog as a finished adult.

If we can offer one piece of advice to the puppy owner, it is this. Do not just assume that your trainer is infallible. You know your puppy better than anyone. If you see something being done that doesn't seem right, stop the trainer and ask what the reasoning is. If you are not satisfied with the answer, tell the trainer to stop. Get another opinion or take time to think it over.

There is no rush to train your pup. A day or two lost in order for you to consider the specific tactics to be used will not hurt the training. On the other hand, if the trainer misjudges and treats your puppy too harshly, it could spell disaster.

If you have properly completed your preliminary work, you should not have a hard time with your puppy now. Your dog already understands the commands and is conditioned to think positively when the command is given. The next step is to increase the dog's attention span and the respect factor.

VERBAL TOOLS (TONE OF VOICE)

By far, the greatest asset in training your dog is your voice. Dogs naturally relate to each other in tones. Low growling noises are used to communicate displeasure or a threat. High-pitched whining noises are used for excited greetings. It is our voice tone and the consistency with which we use it that will ultimately train the dog.

Displeasure: "No"

Displeasure should always be communicated in a low tone of voice. Men usually do not have a hard time with this. Conversely, women may have to practice. We believe that the word "No" should always be associated with correction and that correction should always be associated with "No." Why?

1. Because there will be numerous times when the dog will be beyond your reach and you will correct from a distance. Your dog needs to understand that "No" means to stop immediately.
2. When the correction is perceived as coming only from the leash and collar, it will last only as long as you have the leash and collar on the dog.
3. The dog will develop a negative association with the command when it is given as a correction with a low tone.

Pleasure: "All Right!" "Good Boy!" "That-a-Baby!"

High-pitched tones that express genuine pleasure will be all that most dogs need for motivation. A wagging tail, a high head, a bounce in his step are all good indications that you are praising your dog properly.

Physical praise (petting and hugging) are good rewards as well; however, they should be reserved for an exceptional job or for the end of a training session. The reason behind this is that physical praise is very distracting. The dog will not be able to absorb commands if distracted by touch stimuli.

THE COMMAND

Some of the commands are Heel, Sit, Stay, Come, Down, Stand, Fetch, and Search. The commands themselves should always be neutral or positive. A balanced, even tone of voice is neutral. An upward pitch at the end of a word is deemed positive.

Another way to make the command positive is to associate it with praise. For instance, if the dog is having trouble with the Down command and then all of a sudden gets it right, you might say, "Good Down! Good Down!"

DOG PSYCHOLOGY

Although some human psychology applies to dog training, the dog is a creature of nature and therefore has a unique psychological makeup.

To delve into dog psychology in depth would require a book of its own. The bottom line is that the dog has been set up to learn primarily through association. If you understand this concept, it will make your training experience much easier.

Understanding that what a dog enjoys is likely to be repeated will be the main focus of your training. At the same time, what your dog does not find to be a pleasurable experience will be avoided.

It is either manual (using a leash) or instinctual (using the senses) correction that will be used in association with the undesirable action to achieve a goal.

We must also recognize that we cannot ignore a dog's needs. If they are not met, the dog will act out in an attempt to change things. These needs are:

1. Social contact
2. Play
3. Exercise
4. Food, water and shelter

BREEDING

Sex? Some would question why we did not add sex to this list. We believe that this subject should be addressed separately. We do not wish to imply that dogs need to be sexually active in order to be happy. A dog's sex drive (whether "she" is in season or "he" smells a female in season) is instinctual and set up by nature for reproductive purposes.

Sex is not designed to give pleasure to the dog. A male or female suffers no ill effects if never bred. It is up to humans to separate females in season from males that are frustrated by the scent.

There are numerous unwanted puppies in animal shelters across the country. **The only reason to breed your dog is to better the breed.** This is accomplished by selectively breeding males and females with outstanding qualities.

Breeding Quality Dogs

If you are going to breed your female, take advantage of the fact that you have many males to choose as a stud for her. *Choose a dog with outstanding working ability and show quality.* Research the potential animal's bloodlines and see how they compare with yours.

It is a buyer's market for you once your female has passed all of the criteria set down by her breed (i.e., **OFA** hip X rays, **VWD** tests, eye tests, etc.). Smart breeding means taking the time to check out all of the males available to her.

Too many people breed their females with the dogs next door or use their own "backyard male." This breaks down the breed due to lack of proper selection. The chances of this male and female offsetting one another's faults are slim and none because this type of breeding is not approached in a selective manner.

TO SPAY OR NEUTER?

Many consider spaying or neutering a pet as an end-all to problem-solving. This is a false assumption because few behavior problems actually stem from sexual problems.

The sex hormones, when found in great quantities, can be a factor in aggressive behavior in both males and females. When the behavior is not controllable through training, spaying or neutering may be recommended. Spaying or neutering has a fifty-fifty chance of reducing the drives, and therefore altering behavior. Spaying and neutering slows the metabolism and therefore tends to quiet the overaggressive dog. Neutering is not usually recommended for the dog that is going to be used as a family protection dog because we use these drives to our advantage to teach the dog desired behaviors. After the behaviors are established (at age two or above), and training is complete, you may spay or neuter if necessary. With the family protection dog, spaying or neutering is recommended only for medical reasons. There is no other reason for lessening the drives that you are utilizing in the dog.

It is not true that your male will hop the fence in search of females unless you allow females to come into contact with him regularly. If she is allowed to greet him while in season and then leave a trail for him right back to her home, you will have a problem. Management of your dog is important to prevent this. He should not be in the habit of wandering the neighborhood. Regular walks in the neighborhood where the dog is allowed to lift his leg on plants should also be discouraged as this teaches that this is his territory. He may attempt to leave the yard to remark territory.

YOUR PSYCHOLOGY

Your mind-set is just as important as that of the dog. *Your attitudes toward training flow down the leash as if it were an electric current.* A lack of patience or a frustrated outburst on your part can ruin the dog's confidence and everything you have worked hard for.

Often we remind ourselves and our trainers of one simple fact: **THE DOG YOU ARE TRAINING IS GOING TO MAKE MISTAKES.** If you accept this fact before you begin, you will have the proper mind-set.

It may seem to be an obvious point. One might think if the dog weren't going to make mistakes, why is training needed. The fact of the matter is that once the dog is on the leash, this is the point most likely to be forgotten.

There is a tendency for people to bring their own worries, attitudes and frustrations to the training field. When you lose your patience with the dog, you lose your effectiveness. Because of this we encourage our trainers to tell themselves each dog they bring out is going to make mistakes. Patience is one of the most important assets in training your dog.

SETTING SHORT-TERM GOALS

Everyone has a mental picture of what they want their dog to be like as a finished product—no problem behaviors, the dog is a joy to be around, a member of the family with a job to do (i.e., protection of the family, companion to the children, etc.). Problems occur when people are not patient enough to follow the steps to reach this goal.

The best training programs involve teaching the dog one or two steps at a time. If they are multiple steps, they should be similar in type. An example would be teaching the dog to walk on the leash and to sit at your side, and teaching the dog to come on the leash and to sit in front.

These are similar commands as opposed to teaching the Sit and Stay, and teaching to Come when called. These are opposite behaviors that should be taught separately before working together.

Every time you take the dog out, you should have a goal in mind for that session. The dog's attention span is short dependent on the age and breed. You will only have fifteen to twenty minutes to accomplish this goal which may be to establish the automatic Sit. When you establish this, even if it is for a very short time period, be sure to communicate extreme pleasure in the form of praise. You can then change gears and leave the dog on a high point (i.e., something pleasurable such as a game of toss and fetch).

If you achieve the desired response in a short period of time (ten minutes), you may then decide to train again later for another ten- to twenty-minute period. The amount of time you spend on each training session will be determined by the dog.

A good trainer always finishes a lesson on a high point. It takes experience and good judgment to tell exactly when a dog is doing the best possible in a given session.

ENDING ON A HIGH NOTE

When ending on a high note, three things are accomplished:

1. We keep the dog's enjoyment of the training process at the highest level.
2. We keep the dog's personal confidence level high.
3. We help the dog remember what was done right in order to increase the chance of remembering the correct behavior next time.

THE IMPORTANCE OF BREAK AND PLAYTIME

Break Time

Break time is when the dog wanders freely about an area and may explore the environment by the sense of smell. Your dog may choose this time to urinate or defecate, mark or scratch the ground in this area.

Break time relieves stress. During the transition period between bringing a dog out of the house or kennel, it helps to keep the dog from being preoccupied with the surroundings while training. Also, when the dog is under work pressure (a trial, K-9 security work, etc.), a break allows the dog to relax.

Playtime

Playtime helps your dog release some energy and also to get some exercise. This is also a stress reliever and can be used for the same reasons. Playtime is probably best used after a positive training session as a release. The dog will tend to be at a heightened activity level. Therefore, it is not a good idea to play with the dog and then get a serious attitude for a trial or on the job. In this case, break time is a better release.

DISTRACTIONS

There is a tendency for novice trainers to avoid distractions. Their thinking goes somewhat like this. They believe that it is hard enough to keep the dog's attention and train without having to deal with distractions.

This point is valid for a dog during the first week of training when getting a grasp on the commands. Thereafter, the distraction value should be considered an asset. The distractions will cause you (the trainer) to go into high gear and will make you work.

We believe in attacking the distraction—working on it over and over again until the dog is neutral toward it or ignores it. A good trainer seeks out the dog's weaknesses and works to improve or eliminate them. Say for instance you have a dog that is ball crazy, and the dog's Obedience is very good. He performs a Down Stay for long periods unless a ball rolls by. This could be a potential problem. You need to saturate the problem by putting the dog on a Down Stay and standing alongside. Have an assistant roll a ball and correct the dog if there is a response.

Keep this up until you get the desired response. Each time you get the desired response, you can try more and more tempting (i.e., the ball can roll faster or closer to the dog). Give lots of praise. Release with an "Okay" and give your dog the ball. That way, you will end on a high note.

This exercise teaches the dog three things:

1. To be set up and to remain in place on command.
2. To understand that once given a command, it must be followed until released.
3. Not to worry about the desire for distraction as there may be a reward with play for good behavior.

HOW TO APPLY CORRECTION AND PRAISE

Correction is miles away from abuse. It is used to mold a dog's behavior toward a desired end result. An effective correction should have intensity behind it. It should be quick and sharp like a lightning bolt and should get the dog's attention.

The leash correction should involve the snap of the leash. It is the *quickness* rather than the physical aspect of the correction that will

The dog's attention should be focused on the handler.

make the greatest impact on the dog. The leash should be loose on the neck when the dog is not being corrected. Many people try to keep control by applying pressure at all times. This is wrong and does not teach anything. In fact, holding the leash in this manner promotes the dog pulling into the leash.

Correction must be doled out on a level equal to the stress level of the dog. The main point to be made here is that you need to be aware of the response to your correction. If you don't get your dog's attention, you are not being sharp enough. If you get a ducked head and tucked tail, you are being too sharp. Your desire is to *GET* and *HOLD* your dog's attention.

PRAISE

Your praise should either be excited or soothing. In either case, it should provide the emotion that the dog needs at the time. If you are working an easily excitable dog, you may want to use soothing praise

When this is the case, off-leash work is easily accomplished.

in order to keep an even keel. Excited praise with an excited dog can blow a circuit and make the dog come apart before your eyes. The nervous or fearful dog also needs soothing praise to become calm. Excited praise can make a nervous dog flighty.

Excitable praise is good for the aloof, stubborn or slow dog who may need a squad of cheerleaders just to be a bit bouncy. A good trainer consistently adjusts the level of correction and praise according to the dog being worked.

WHAT YOU ARE LOOKING FOR FROM THE DOG

What you are seeking is the dog's respect and attention for you. A good working dog looks at and is constantly aware of the owner. You do not want your dog to be afraid not to look at you to the point of running into a pole or falling into a ditch. At the same time, you want the dog to keep an eye on you in case you make a quick signal or change direction.

RULES FOR OBEDIENCE TRAINING PREPARATION

1. Do not feed the dog immediately prior to training.
2. Keep the dog confined in a crate or run at least a couple of hours prior to training. This will heighten the dog's willingness to come out and work.
3. If you will be training in a place without water, bring a dish and water.

YOUR ULTIMATE GOAL

The ultimate goal is to have as a finished product a dog that, without the benefit of a leash or collar, will do as you ask without need of correction and with a positive attitude. Right?

That's the ultimate goal. That's what everyone wants.

There are steps to getting there. It's a safe bet that any dog you see that you would consider to be in this category has had the benefit of someone's time and patience. Following are the steps:

1. The process is one of building willingness to work through motivations (i.e., verbal and physical praise, food and toy reward). At the same time, polish the performance by using correction (compulsion) to the degree necessary. A combination of these tools will turn out the best finished product.
2. Put less and less emphasis on leash control in the 30-foot and light leash phases. Ultimately, eliminate the leash for use of the tab.
3. Eliminate the tab and ultimately the collar while increasing the reward to bridge the gap.
4. Increase verbal praise, decrease obvious toy or food in training until the very end.
5. Work on nonverbal commands using reward and praise in bursts from the trainer at the end of each session. Wean the dog from the voice.

The dog usually attains this level by two to three years of age. This is largely due to maturity and the volume of time it takes to truly condition the dog. You can catch a bear easier with honey than with a rope.

DOG AND OWNER SYNERGY

Definition of synergy: The action of two or more substances, organs or organisms achieving an effect of which each is individually incapable.

The most important aspect of your training is the basic love relationship between you and your dog. It looks so easy when a dynamic duo of dog and owner are in sync—the dog performs precisely as desired with confidence. The handler has practiced enough to have confidence in the dog. A pair like this actually radiates pride and confidence.

At this point, you need to dedicate yourself and your energies to that furry face (your dog) with a positive attitude. Dogs do not get trained by themselves so this must be understood from the onset.

Typical Pitfalls

1. "I do not have the time." We have all used this excuse at some time. This translates into "I don't want to make the time for that." This is a matter of priorities. People need to be realistic with regard to where they spend their time. Owning a dog takes time. **IF YOU DO NOT HAVE THE TIME, DO NOT GET A DOG!**

   There are courses you can take with professional trainers where the trainer does the first half of the training for you. Provided you have selected your trainer carefully, these are excellent for the dog and you.

   This type of course is recommended for busy professional couples, older people with physical limitations and people with particularly difficult dogs.

   The point is that you will need to be personally involved in the training. Even with kennel training, a good trainer will work with you and your dog afterward at your home, and you will need to practice your homework daily for a few weeks.

   You must spend sufficient time with your dog in order to get good results. If you expect to train your dog for personal protection, time spent is a necessity.

2. "Realistic expectations." Because you are a team, you must make sure that you are very involved with every aspect of the dog. For instance, it will not work if your mate feeds, plays

with, grooms and otherwise spends time with the dog and all you do is train. You need to have a personal relationship with the dog.

Set realistic goals for you and your dog. Realize that if you just want a companion dog, you will be putting in two to three months of training. If a companion/protection dog is your goal, you will be in training one to two years. If you wish to compete in European sport, you are looking at three to six years of intense training.

3. Let's compare dog training to a fitness program. If your goal is to lose five or ten pounds, you may decide to work out now and then to stay at your desired weight. The mind-set for basic Obedience is the same. Consistently teach the desired commands and then maintain them on a random, but regular basis.

On the other hand, if your goal is to teach a personal protection dog, this is better compared to a person in a military fitness program. The work is much more demanding so the training needs to be a constant half hour to one hour per day so as to maintain a state of readiness.

4. "I can't afford it." It is common to hear people say, "I can't afford to spend the money." Here again, we come back to priorities. People spend money on whatever is important to them.

What price do you put on the dog? Is your dog only worth what you paid? Is your baby only worth what it cost for delivery? Of course not, because you love them. What price can you affix to a member of your family?

5. What is the reduction of stress in your daily life worth to you? Does it make a difference in your attitude when you arrive home after a long day of work to find your yard destroyed? What is it worth to you to come home without this problem?

In the case of the family protection dog, what is it worth to you to have the peace of mind knowing your dog is at home protecting your family or waiting in your car or next to you at the ATM machine late at night? How do you put a price tag on these things?

One of the problems with justifying money spent on protection is that in many cases, you do not know when it has worked in your behalf. Since a good deal of protection is the deterrent factor, you may never know if the presence of your dog kept away a would-be assailant.

Sometimes various factors (i.e., statistics) can point out to you that you have managed to beat the odds and maybe that your dog is part of the reason. At times, good examples present themselves such as the following real-life story.

We have been training Rottweilers for the last twelve years for a very nice family who owns a jewelry store. Throughout the years, we have trained six Rottweilers for this couple and their two grown children for their protection.

We were first contacted by Ted and Mary (not their real names) because they had been held up and robbed in their store three times in three months. The last time, they had guns held to their heads and were tied up in the back room of the store.

After this, they were determined to do what they could to protect themselves. They decided on dogs. Their daughters gave them a Rottweiler and they called us. This was in 1980. By 1983, Lizzy had scared away her share of malcontents. She was relied on and loved a great deal.

Unfortunately, Lizzy died prematurely of liver failure and we were called in to train her daughter, Lexy, and another male dog named Astro. This was a beautiful working pair. At one point, they interrupted a confrontation that was just beginning in the store. Upon seeing the dogs poised and ready to strike, the bad guy quickly retreated.

In 1987, Ted and Mary experienced a temporary separation. Ted left and opened another store, leaving Mary with the dogs. He was hit the first month he was in the new store without the dogs. Ted firmly believes that the seven years he conducted business without a robbery was due almost entirely to the presence of the dogs.

As with most desirable things in life the protection dog requires a commitment of time and money. This commitment should be well thought out before the purchase of the dog in order to be fair to everyone concerned.

Proper application of the training collar.

CHAPTER X

Obedience Training
(4–8 Months)

OBEDIENCE begins with five basic commands: Heel, Sit, Stay, Come and Down. These commands are the basic foundation of training that any dog should know. After teaching the basics, it is desirable to go on with more advanced training such as retrieving, jumping, scent tests, Sit in motion, Down in motion, Down on Recall, and so on. You can accomplish this because all Obedience stems from the five basic commands.

EQUIPMENT

- 6-foot leather or nylon leash
- 30-foot-long line
- 10-inch tab
- Small-link German steel choke chain
- Optional: Prong collar (with older, stronger, assertive dogs)

Collars and leashes should always be purchased with the size and strength of the dog in mind. A large personal protection dog should be worked on a one-inch-wide leash, preferably with a brass clip.

Choke chains must be put on correctly to work properly. We

recommend small-link choke chains because they release easier than the large oblong links. When the dog is on your left-hand side at the Heel position, the chain should come over the top of the neck and down through the *O* ring. If you hold the ring in your hand, you should be holding the end of the letter *P*.

OBEDIENCE COMMANDS—Level 1 (4–6 Months)
Five Commands—6-Foot Leash

Heel

Teaching Heel will be much easier if the dog is already leash broken. Start with the dog on your left side and hold the leash across your body in your right hand. Your left hand should be loosely holding the leash over the top.

Start by patting your leg and stepping off with your left foot. Command "Baron, Heel." Begin to encourage with "Good, Thata baby!" If the dog pulls or balks, give him a quick jerk as a correction with a "No." Keep walking and encouraging him.

Make "about" turns to maintain attention and tell Baron that he is going with you. When you stop, pull up with your right hand and push down carefully on the dog's rear end, saying "Sit." Praise once the dog is in this position. The easiest way to teach that the idea is to stay with you in this particular position, is to walk quickly to keep the dog's attention.

If your dog's head is not up and eyes are not looking at you, most likely the problem has to do with your intensity—both verbal and physical. When the dog is learning, you should be talking constantly so the dog always knows what is right or wrong.

If you run into problems, try to motivate the dog with food or a toy. Take it a little at a time—three or four steps—before stopping to praise.

Sit

There are three different versions of the *Sit* command that the dog needs to know:

Step 1

1. Sit when told to, regardless of position
2. Sit in front (on recall)
3. Automatic Sit at the Heel command

110

Handler with the proper leash position.

Directing the dog into the proper position is a key in the beginning steps of training.

Lisa guides Jacki O' (a Bouvier des Flandres) into the correct sitting position.

Shown is the proper technique for correction on the Sit command.

By now, you should have already taught what Sit means by using food (Chapter VI). Transfer this to a little game using a toy. After you know that the dog understands the concept, you can move to polish the performance.

Step 2

Polishing the performance means adding correction to your training. By now, your dog knows to plant his or her rear end on the ground when you command "Sit."

The next step would be to correct with "No," and a sharp jerk on the training collar if the dog doesn't follow through. When your dog comes to you, there should be an automatic Sit in front of you. On the Heel command, the dog should sit automatically when you stop. If not, just apply the correction with a "No."

Step 3

Now that the command is understood and the dog knows that you will give a correction, you can begin to use the toy less and less. The

112

Introducing the Down command.

After the dog understands the Down command, the foot correction can be applied. As soon as the dog complies, the pressure should be released.

Finally, the dog should receive lavish praise.

toy is a motivator; however, you do not want the dog to become dependent on it. Hopefully, you have developed such a good relationship at this point that your puppy will work just as happily for your praise.

Down

The Down command tends to be the most difficult of all because in the dog's mind it is a submissive command. *The older the dog is when you begin to teach this command, the harder it will be to teach.* This is especially true when you are working the high-stress-level protection candidate.

It is best to start with an eight-week-old puppy with food reward conditioning. If you have not done this, begin with the older pup using food (described in Chapter VI).

When you progress to the toy, there is only one way to use reward properly. Once on the Down, give the dog the toy as a reward for the Down and leave your dog on a Stay with the toy.

For some dogs, this allows you to lengthen the Stay because the dog is comfortable holding or chewing on the toy. For other dogs that become active with the toy and scoot across the ground, you will have to eliminate the toy altogether.

Stay

Stay was not worked on during puppy training because of the dog's short attention span. Even though the pup has matured to the point of being able to learn the Stay command, we still need to realize that four to six months of age is not mature enough to hold this position for a long period of time. We need to ensure short-term successes now in order to build up to longer periods in the future.

Start with the pup at the Heel position. Give the desired command to Sit or Down. Do not use the toy or food on this command, as your dog will be motivated to come toward you. Signal a Stay, holding the palm of your left hand firmly in front of the dog's nose.

1. Step out in front of the dog (about two to three feet).
2. Begin to walk slowly in a half circle around your dog, right foot first.
3. Use soothing praise and frequently show the hand signal.

Be ready to step in and correct quickly if the dog starts to move.

The hand signal for Stay should be clear to the dog.

Sit/Stay

1. Correct in an upward manner for a Sit/Stay. Quickly place your dog back in the original spot.
2. Give him the signal with your palm up again.
3. Step out again and begin your half circle again.

Down Stay

1. For the Down Stay, step in and step on the leash as the dog is getting up. This will anchor the dog to the spot.
2. Reach for the leash above where it is anchored.
3. Correct the dog in a downward manner.
4. Once the dog is down, give the signal to Stay by showing the palm of your hand.
5. Step back out and begin your half circle again.

ANCHORING THE DOG

If you have a particularly difficult time with the dog moving toward you on the Stay, you may want to "anchor" for a while until the dog gets the idea. You can anchor by using a tree or post of some sort.

Using a 30-foot-long line, wrap it around the post or tree and connect the other end to your dog's collar. The line should go around the post at the same level the collar is on the dog. Thus, if this is the Sit/Stay, the line will be between two to three feet from the ground.

On the Down Stay, the line will be under the dog at ground level. To the dog, you will still seem to be controlling the leash. If the dog tries to move toward you, it will be impossible. Your dog will be automatically corrected with any momentum when coming to you.

Come

The Recall or Come command should be introduced during free movement. Do not call a dog from a Stay position at this point. If this mistake is made, it will take much longer to teach not to break a Stay.

We want to emphasize the Come command. This is because it is a key to protecting yourself from excessive liability as well as assuring your dog's safety. The food and toy reward works well here because it motivates the dog to come quickly.

In competition of the AKC and Schutzhund variety, the dog must come front and sit, and upon command then proceed to the Heel position to finish the exercise.

In French and Dutch sports, the dog immediately proceeds to the Heel position. This is the way we prefer to train personal protection dogs if they are not going to compete in AKC trials or Schutzhund events. Beyond this difference, the command is basically taught the same way.

1. The dog is free wandering and sniffing around, not on any command. The release word "Okay" should have been given.
2. If you have been using food in the puppy stage, your dog will already associate coming to you with reward. If not, begin with food. Call the dog to you and wave a toy.
3. As your dog comes to you, to have the dog sit properly, do the following:
    Sit in front—hold the toy (or food) in front of you. Say "Sit" and after he has been sitting for five or six seconds, give the toy and praise.

Move backward on the Recall to get the dog to come with enthusiasm.

When the dog sits in front, attention should be focused on you.

The military-style finish requires the dog to swing from the front position to your left Heel position without moving behind you.

Sit at Heel—As the dog comes to you, step back and bring the toy around the back of you, right in front of his nose, with the dog following the toy behind your back. Bring the toy up as he comes into the Heel position and say "Sit." Wait five or six seconds and give the toy and praise!

After your dog has learned to follow the toy, you can move on to the next step, keeping the toy on you (in your belt or pocket). Call the dog to you and into the proper position and sit. If the dog does not follow through use a leash correction. Once the dog has complied, give the toy as a reward.

Be sure you are patient and do not go too quickly through these steps. Depending on the age of the dog you are training, each step can span a period of days or weeks.

PAIRING YOUR EXERCISES

Training will go much smoother if you pair up exercises that complement one another. For example, the first lesson taught could be walking at the Heel position and Come when called. They are of the same concept—staying near the handler and sitting when the dog stops.

For instance, these commands are much easier to learn together than the concepts of Stay and Come. Sit and Down can be paired together as they are also similar commands.

Stay should be taught separately after the Sit and Down are well established. There are many other Obedience commands that can be taught, such as:

- Stand for Examination
- Figure 8
- Down on Recall
- Stay on Recall
- Retrieve over High Jump
- Sit in motion
- Stand in motion
- Down in motion
- Food refusal
- Scent Discrimination
- Change of positions at a distance
- Broad Jump
- Stay with handler out of sight

The French-style Recall leaves out the Sit in front and requires that the dog come around immediately to the Heel position. This is the style of choice for the personal protection dog.

- Obstacle work
- Directed Retrieves
- Send aways

Due to limited space and since this book is based on the family protection dog, we have chosen only to explain those that can be applied directly to this objective:

1. Stand for Examination will make it easier for the groomer or veterinarian to work on or to examine the dog.
2. Stay and Down on Recall help to ensure the dog's safety because he can stop in case of a car or other danger.
3. Food Refusal helps to poison-proof the dog and is an addition to the methods used in Chapter XVI.
4. Obstacle Work helps the dog's confidence level, as well as teaches him how to negotiate obstacles if he needs to in the course of his work.
5. Stay (with handler out of sight) teaches the dog to be reliable when the handler leaves.

These will be covered in Chapter XI, Beyond the Basics.

30-FOOT-LONG LINE WORK

After the five basic Obedience commands have been covered and you are happy with the dog's performance on the 6-foot leash, you are ready to proceed to the long line. The long line is used to establish your control at a distance while at the same time allowing the dog more freedom.

This is not a new concept. You most likely have used this piece of equipment to give your puppy break time before this point. You have probably called your dog a few times using this as well.

You will now use this piece of equipment to build up your distance work. Your goal will be to make the long line as insignificant as possible in the dog's eyes. In reality, it is a very significant piece of equipment to you as it allows you to have control of the dog's actions at a distance.

Heel

Begin by putting the bulk of the line in your right hand. This is away from the dog's line of vision on your left. Drop the line behind your back and over your right shoulder only. Now it is out of sight even on your left.

Keep your left hand swinging free as you do your heeling exercise, and make turns often. Try to use only your voice for correction and encouragement. If he gets way out of line, reach back to the line and give a quick jerk. Show the dog, if need be, that you still have the ability for correction.

Turns

Practice a lot of squared turns to the left and right using this. If the dog tends to lead, make more frequent left and about turns in order to check the pace. If necessary, jerk just as you make the turn to keep your dog alert.

The slow dog will need about turns and right turns to keep up. Instead of applying correction into the turn, you will apply motivation and encouragement in the form of your voice and a toy.

Come Command

Now the Recall command will involve more distractions (i.e., someone talking, offering food or a toy, etc.)

Step 1

Call the dog away and give a chance to respond. Give a "No" command and jerk if you get no response. Praise into the proper position. Praise only after a complete Sit at the Heel position.

Step 2

Now you want to reach a point with the dog where the line is not so obvious. To do this, leave the line on the ground and call, using only your voice and reward if necessary for encouragement. If necessary, pick up the line only to make the correction.

- Try not to rely on the line because it will not be there later on.
- Work through Sit and Down Stay on the long line before going to Step 3.

Step 3

You have completed both the Sit and Down Stay on long line and Step 2 of Recall before going to this step.

Recall from the Stay

Put the dog on a Sit/Stay and move to the end of the line. Call the dog to come after about a minute. Give a gentle tug and encouragement, showing that this is okay.

From here, finish your exercise with praise and reward. Recall from the Down Stay is the same. We suggest you do this second, because it is easier to pull a dog from a Sit than from a Down.

Sit and Down Stay

With the help of your long line, you can begin to teach the dog to Stay at a distance with more distractions. Work your way slowly away from the dog until you are accomplishing Sit and Down Stays at 30 feet.

Distractions

Distractions are very important at this juncture of training. Do not go crazy throwing everything but the kitchen sink at the dog. Give one test at a time. Always be ready to correct when providing distractions.

Go to the dog and always give a quick jerk with your correction, saying "No." If you do not jerk, correction will quickly lose its meaning. Possible distractions include:

1. Other dogs working in the area
2. Other people milling about
3. People talking to him (no commands)
4. Loud noises—dropping boards, pounding nails, gunshots, trash cans banging, etc.
5. Throwing balls, oranges, rocks, sticks, etc.
6. Food thrown near him (not at him)
7. Cats, rabbits, squirrels, livestock, etc.
8. Road noise—cars, trucks, etc.

OBEDIENCE COMMANDS—Level 2 (6–8 Months)

Off-Leash Obedience

You are ready to work for your off-leash control when you find yourself rarely having to correct the dog with the leash.

Light Leash

The first step will be to use a very light leash, one that is not much heavier than a parachute cord. This is the type you would use on a Toy breed. With small dogs, we use dental floss. With large protection breeds, we use a Toy breed leash.

Drop the leash and proceed through your commands as if the leash weren't there. It is there for you to step on in order to anchor the dog. Do not step on it by accident. This can set your training back.

Keep your motivation high in this level of your training. Read your dog to know if you need to use voice, a toy or food for motivation. By this stage of your training, it is preferable that the dog is voice motivated. If you need more motivation, do not hesitate to use it.

Tab

Next you will use the handle or the tab, a short piece of leash or handle loop no more than 10 inches in length. This allows you to correct when necessary, while at the same time having the dog off of the leash.

The reason you need the tab is that quick solid correction must be an option during this phase of training. Reaching down to find the *O* ring of the collar can be both time-consuming and painful.

Run through all five commands on the tab. Do this in a safe place where your dog cannot escape or get hit by a car. Remember to use whatever motivation is necessary.

Start working the dog at close proximity to you and work your way out to a comfortable distance. Always remember that you are free to regress to any of the former steps. *Just because the dog can now work off leash does not mean that you will never again use a leash.* The same goes for the long line and the light line.

The leash law demands the use of a leash in public places for everyone's safety. It is also good practice for the dog. The long line allows you to keep a distance and at the same time exercise safety.

Practice your doors and boundaries with the long line, light line

On the off-leash Recall, the dog should now show the same enthusiasm without your movement being necessary.

The AKC Finish has the dog sit in front and then move to the Finish either from behind or in military style.

and tab as well. The light line and the tab should be used for the Place command.

The difficulty in getting the dog successfully off leash will depend on a number of factors. In general, the younger the dog when you began conditioning, the easier it will be to work off leash.

The Collar-Wise Dog

Dogs usually become collar-wise (meaning that they obey only when the collar is on) due to our concern for safety. We usually put the collar on for training and then take it off when we are finished so that he will not accidently choke himself in the kennel or elsewhere.

The problem here is that the dog thinks, ''There's no collar on me so that means I don't have to work.'' To break this cycle, we must first leave the collar on 100 percent of the time for a two-month period. This period will include the time when we are teaching the advanced work.

We are continuously breaking a cycle and we must accept the risk we take and minimize the dangers by eliminating everything we can find that the dog may become hung up on. This is especially true when the dog is in the crate for safety while we are away.

CHAPTER XI

Beyond the Basics
(8–16 Months)

ADVANCE OBEDIENCE—PREPROTECTION
AND AGILITY

This is a very important stage in your dog's life. It is also a very critical part of the training process. This is a transitional phase for your dog because this is the age of sexual maturity. Somewhere in this age range, your bitch will come into heat for the first time. The male dog's cue to maturity is that he will begin to lift his leg.

As a result of physiological change, mature dogs will become a little more serious and defense-minded. How you handle the relationship with your dog at this juncture of the training process is critical to your success.

Start thinking of yourself as a coach. Your desire should be to instill confidence and to cheer your dog on. When you see regression, adjust your techniques in order to get your dog moving forward again.

Your goals at this time should be to:

1. Strengthen the bond between you and your dog.
2. Build the dog's confidence with preprotection training.
3. Build confidence by exposure to various noises; clatter sticks, gunfire, etc.

Agility helps build confidence.

4. Add to your basic on- and off-leash Obedience with advanced Obedience and Agility work that will strengthen confidence and communication.
5. Give yourself an attitude check. Remember that although the dog may be getting large, the dog's brain is still young. Do not make the mistake of expecting too much too soon. You still have a year of training (given that everything goes right) before your great expectations will be realized. You do not

have control of when your dog matures; however, you do have control of when your dog becomes trained.

1. STRENGTHEN THE BOND—YOU ARE A TEAM

One of the best ways to strengthen your bond with your dog is to spend time together. For those who spend a lot of time training their dog, this is an ideal time to take a week or two off and just be together.

- Go on a vacation.
- Ride around in the car.
- Get a new toy and play.
- Go to the mountains or the beach.
- Bicycle ride together.
- Take walks and discover new surroundings.

2. BUILD THE DOG'S CONFIDENCE WITH PREPROTECTION TRAINING

You need to work the young dog in the prey mode. Begin to play harder with the tug, turn the dog's head from side to side, taking care not to overturn or turn too vigorously. Your dog *must always* win. You can intensify the movement, the angles of the turns and the distance of the travel between dog and decoy.

Work with your trainer now with the puppy tug, the puppy sleeve or the protection suit pants. Whatever you choose at this age should be determined by two factors: the goals for the dog's future and the animal's maturity level.

If one of your goals is a **ZTP** (a breed suitability test) or a Schutzhund title, you will want to go with a sleeve. Likewise, if you wish to compete in French Ring Sport, you should stick with a French Ring suit.

The advantage you have if the animal is strictly a personal protection dog for the home and family is that you have options. You can teach the dog to be an upper body biter only, using the sleeve to train before going to the jacket. On the other hand, if full body biting is what you desire, you should teach ''legs first'' (using the pants) and add the jacket later for upper body bites. Keep in mind that it is more natural for the dog to bite the upper body.

The young pup can learn to play with the tug casually with the owner, and when he is more confident, a second party can begin to serve as a decoy through play.

If the dog is not mature enough to have a good strong bite on the tug, do not even attempt work on a sleeve or pants. Some breeds mature into their drives early while others are slower to blossom. Your trainer will let you know when the time is right to advance to a puppy sleeve or pants. Remember to make sure that these sessions are short and fun for the dog.

Step 1
Equipment:

- Tie out line (rubber stretch line with brass buckles)
- Protection collar (two inches wide)
- Harness (optional)

Drag the prey object (i.e., tug, sleeve or pants) in front of the dog with a leash. Drag it in a straight line—just out of reach—so that your dog can chase it. Encourage and cheer the dog on. When Buck does catch the prey, praise and let him run with it. It is desirable to keep your leash around your shoulder so that when it is appropriate, you can let the dog carry the prey away. Do this by snapping the leash on and taking the dog off the tie out.

Once you are successful with this step, you will want to advance to Step 2. Proceed slowly through each of these steps. Some dogs can

When the pup is more mature, serious work becomes more intense.

Finally, the suit is introduced. The pants or the jacket may be first, depending on your desired target.

advance through each step in days, while others take weeks, even months. We encourage you to be patient.

Step 2

The next step is to put on the sleeve or the pants. The sleeve is easy to let go of to give to the dog. The legs are not as easy. Choose to use a jambier (leg sleeve) or start out with only one leg in the pants as we usually do. As long as the decoy's shoes can slip out of the leg, he or she can take the bite. When ready, the decoy can lean out away from the dog and slip off the pants.

In either case, you must get the dog's attention to the desired point of impact. This is accomplished by moving the object back and forth quickly in front of the dog's line of vision, just barely out of reach. You want the dog to jump out toward the arm or leg to try and bite it.

Periodically, the sleeve or leg should swing close enough for the dog to believe that he or she can make contact. Eventually when the dog is at the peak of excitement, the decoy will step in and take the bite. A short fight without undue pressure should follow by the release of the prey object, whether it be a sleeve or the pants. This should be practiced until the fight is longer and the bite is solid. The dog should be biting hard with full mouth.

The handler can help the bite by holding the line tight when the dog bites. This will help the dog to bite down hard or lose the grip. A loose line will cause mouthing as well as release and bite tendencies where the dog does not hold on.

Begin to teach the "Out" now without correction. After the handler releases the sleeve or pants and the dog has them in his mouth reach down and grab the leather collar and pull the dog up on the hind legs. This will eventually become uncomfortable, and the dog will drop the equipment. As this happens, say "OUT." Every time you do this, you are teaching what the word means.

Step 3

It is easier for a dog to bite someone who is running away than it is face to face. When biting sufficiently hard on the tie out line, the dog should be taken off the line and put on the leash connected to the police collar (2 inches wide) with a heavy brass snap. We highly recommend the use of brass snaps because other snaps are known to break.

The decoy will come out with the equipment and agitate the dog

Allowing the dog to chase and bite the jacket must be followed by a brief tug . . .

Next the jacket is slipped . . .

The decoy then rewards the dog with the jacket and the dog is left with her reward to savor her victory. This builds confidence.

133

to high intensity. When the decoy says "Go" or signals, the handler releases the dog with the bite command "Foss." When the dog gets to the decoy, the handler will make sure that the leash is tight enough that when the decoy slips the equipment, the dog will go no further. The dog will gain more and more confidence each time. The dog has scared and chased the decoy down and was rewarded with an article. Therefore, the dog wins!

3. BUILD CONFIDENCE BY EXPOSURE TO VARIOUS NOISES (I.E., CLATTER STICKS, WHIPS, GUNFIRE, ETC.)

Introduce noises slowly and at a distance. Gradually bring them closer and, within reason, let them get louder. It is wise to let the dog hear noises at random. Have someone create a noise distraction during Obedience work or preprotection training off and on leash. Be inventive.

Get the dog used to seeing sticks and being rubbed with them. The dog should also be made aware of the sound they make in a nonstressful setting. If you find that your dog is sensitive to something in particular, concentrate on this area. Make sure your dog is slowly desensitized to whatever it is by association and positive experiences.

4. ADD TO YOUR ON- AND-OFF LEASH OBEDIENCE WITH ADVANCED OBEDIENCE AND AGILITY WORK

Sit and Down Stay (with handler out of sight)

Your dog should be able to perform the Sit and Down Stay off leash and for several minutes at a time. We will now work on the dog's ability to do this with you out of sight.

Start with the long line stretched out 30 feet toward the blind (hidden area) that you are in. This way, if your dog moves, you can catch the line quickly. Move into the blind at first for only thirty seconds. Increase the time (thirty seconds at a time) until you are doing this for several minutes.

Next, you can do this with just a light leash until you never have to correct. When you must correct, make sure you take the dog back to the exact starting spot with a swift jerk. Aggressively say "No"

Food refusal aids in poison-proofing and practices discipline. This dog's handler hides in the blind in the background.

anytime a mistake is made. When there are no mistakes on a light line, remove the leash completely.

Down Stay with Food Refusal and Distractions

As previously stated, in order to teach the new concept, we will first go back to the basics with a 6-foot leash.

Put the dog on a Down Stay and squat alongside. Have a friend approach and talk to the dog. Correct if the dog tries to stand up. Praise if the dog stays, saying "Good dog. Good Stay."

When you are just beginning, work on typical distractions such as the person's approach, talking, clapping hands, throwing stones, rolling balls, and so on.

When you have distraction-proofed the dog, try food. Slivers of hot dogs are tempting. Have the person approach and begin to toss hot dogs just out of the dog's reach. Each time the dog shows interest, make a speedy correction. Praise the dog for compliance.

As the dog gets better at coping with distractions, you can begin to move back and away. The dog knows what you want, and you do not need to hover. Move in deliberate steps. Stand alongside your dog. Next, step back 6 feet, then 10, 15, until you can go behind the blind and the dog will still refuse food or any other distraction.

Stay and Down on Recall

By now, your dog is used to coming swiftly when you call. But what would you do if you called and suddenly realized that it was dangerous for your dog to come to you at that moment (i.e., a car is coming). The Stay or Down on Recall could be a lifesaver.

Begin by using the 6-foot leash and practice backing up as the dog comes forward. At any point you choose, command the dog to Stay and step forward with your palm extended. Praise the dog for staying. Correct in a backward action if your dog continues to come toward you.

The same goes for the Down. Back up and give the Down command. Praise for response. Correct using your foot on the leash nearer the dog if necessary, to teach the dog to hit the ground on command. Eventually, you can move back farther by using the long line. Ultimately lose the leash altogether.

For a dog that comes running fast you may have to use a double line and have a second party stop the dog when the command is given.

Sit and Down from a Distance

The Sit and Down from a distance is very similar to the Down on Recall.

Begin with the dog on the end of the 6-foot leash. Step in front and give the command to Down with a downward motion. Praise and/ or correct as necessary. Always correct in the direction that you want the dog to go. You will find that if you take a step forward, the dog will be more likely to Down. If you take a step backward, the dog will be more likely to sit. Work your way backward in distance using the long line until your dog can do it at 30 feet.

When you take off the line at first, remain close and gradually work your way back again to a 30-foot distance.

Stand for Examination

The Stand for Examination is necessary when the dog is in competition, but it also has its practical purposes for grooming or examining the dog. One of the easiest ways to teach this is to slip leash the dog just before the hindquarters. Make sure the leash is not too tight or the dog will panic.

From the Heel position, tell the dog to Heel and take two steps. After two steps, make a half turn to your left, command the dog to

The Stand for Examination can be taught first with 2 leashes and at close proximity to the dog.

After a time, the handler moves to the end of the leash using the Stay command.

Stand. As you do so, pull both ends of the leash (the one on the neck and the one on the hindquarters) until they are firmly holding the dog up. Praise the dog for standing. Repeat this process three times each and try to finish before the dog is stressed. Repeat the Stand command with "Good Stand" when you get the correct response.

You can also reinforce the Stand command with treats. This is especially good for the dog who may be shown in the conformation ring.

Obstacles—Agility—Slippery Surfaces

An additional confidence builder is the Agility course. This consists of catwalks, barrel jumps and tunnels that the dog must learn to negotiate.

You can find these obstacles at a trainer's field or you can be creative and use a slide on a playground, hedges, or bales of straw. Be careful to make sure that the dog does not get hurt. Like a human being, a dog needs to warm up all muscles before attempting to jump. Take it slowly and use encouragement. Do not expect your dog to master everything at once. Add in a new obstacle only after an old one is no longer stressful to the dog.

If you choose to use a motivator such as a jute toy or ball as a reward, the dog may be more willing and less apt to worry about the

Even the heavy-bodied Rottweiller can do Agility work.

Dogs trained in advanced Obedience should be fully controllable around distractions.

obstacle that blocks or comes before the reward. Make sure that jumps are started low and gradually increased in height or length. As a dog gets older and into serious protection work, we will want to use some of these Agility tools again in bite work.

Every time the dog is asked to jump over an object, a command such as ''Hup'' should be issued. Likewise, a command such as ''Under'' can be issued anytime there is something to go under such as a tunnel, fence or bushes.

Your dog should also get used to slippery or uneven surfaces. You do not want the dog to be ineffective because of never having been on a slick floor or stairs. Exposure is important. In advanced protection work, we will come back to slippery surfaces.

5. ATTITUDE CHECK

This is the time to do an attitude check on both you and your dog. Are you having fun yet?! You should be.

Sure, there's a lot of effort being put forth by you. If you're doing a good job, you should feel good about it. Your dog should be happy too.

If you and your dog are stressed out, you are putting too much pressure on both of you. It is so important to remember to *BE PA-*

TIENT! Do not blow it by getting angry. Your dog will eventually work to its potential as long as your attitude remains positive.

Different breeds can do this work at various ages. For example, German Shepherd Dogs and Doberman Pinschers tend to mature at a somewhat slower pace than Rottweilers or Belgian Malinois. Bear in mind that this is a generality as every dog is an individual. All top competition dogs are three to six years old. The older the dog, the more practice and experience the dog has had. Of course the inevitable day comes when performance will begin to slip due to age and/or illness.

With most dogs, you should be ready to get serious with the protection work at about one year of age. You will be able to tell a change in the dog's attitude. The awareness level will go up, the dog will display less insecure behavior and will begin to scent mark.

This brings us to the end of the first year of training which marks a new transition period. From here on, the work is serious. If you have somehow avoided seeking a professional for guidance, we highly suggest you start shopping for a good, licensed trainer *now*.

You cannot decoy for your own dog. If you get a nonprofessional to do this, you are putting both yourself and your dog at great risk. If you were to make a mistake, the decoy could be seriously injured. This can be compared to learning safety procedures for a firearm . . . you need to know and understand safety procedures with the protection dog.

CHAPTER XII

Handler Awareness

ANY PROFESSIONAL who has worked with dogs and owners for a significant period of time is aware that 90 percent of problems with dogs are really *people problems*. In general, dogs are much more willing to learn and adapt than people are.

Many get into the business of professional dog training because they love dogs. A year or two later, they are burned out and the typical response is, "I couldn't deal with the mentality of the people."

In the field of dog training, we do run into all kinds—both humans and K-9s. If trainers could just deal with the dogs by themselves, our jobs would be fun and easy. Unfortunately, the success of our training programs is more directly linked to how well we train humans rather than the animals.

It is imperative that anyone giving thought to owning a protection dog be aware of the responsibilities and potential liabilities of doing so. This is not meant to discourage the reader, but rather to make sure an owner is qualified.

Realistically, anyone who drives a motor vehicle must comprehend that they are dealing with something that could cause serious injury or even death under the wrong circumstances. *In doing so, we must take stock of ourselves and our abilities to handle such responsibilities.*

The following are examples of people who should **not own** a companion/protection dog:

- People who want the dog to work for them, but do not have time to give to the dog
- People who only want the dog for protection but really do not like dogs in general
- People who are afraid of dogs by nature
- People who have physical limitations and, if necessary, cannot hold the dog
- People who let their dogs wander freely in the neighborhood
- Criminals looking to protect drugs or stolen property
- Gang members who want to intimidate others
- People who are regularly intoxicated or high on drugs
- People who want to show off to others

The best owners of protection dogs are those who are *aware* of the dogs at all times and what their dogs are paying attention to. This factor alone will prevent 90 percent of all accidents. Accidents with dogs are not limited to accidental bites. More than likely it would be prevention of dog fights, killing of small animals, eating poisonous plants, getting hung up on something, etc. Simply stated, *awareness is the key* in all of these cases.

RESPONSIBILITIES OF DOG OWNERSHIP

It has been stated elsewhere in this book, but it is worth repeating again—dog ownership carries with it some basic moral and legal responsibilities.

Morally, you are responsible for your dog's basic health, safety and welfare. Just as with a child, the dog is innocent, and doesn't have the ability to tell you when something hurts or that it feels lonely or afraid. You have to care enough to pay close attention to your dog's needs. If your dog is ill, hurt or stressed, he or she is not going to train well. Following the management procedures set forth in this book will help to prevent many of the problems that might occur otherwise.

LEGAL RESPONSIBILITY

It is your legal responsibility to always maintain control of your dog. This is for the dog's safety as well as that of other people and dogs. Dogs running loose are a menace to society. It is inconsiderate to let your dog run free when other people or animals are present. The dangers are numerous to your dog and to others. They include:

- Dog gets hit by a car
- Driver gets in accident trying to avoid a dog
- Dog attacks another dog
- Dog attacks child
- Dog attacks adult
- Dog attacks livestock
- Dog is bitten by a snake or other animal
- Dog is shot with a gun or arrow
- Dog is picked up by animal control
- Dog is stolen

We have seen or heard of all of these examples. It never ceases to amaze us how people think that they are doing the dog a favor by letting it run loose. This "freedom mentality" is similar to allowing your two-year-old toddler to walk around the neighborhood unsupervised.

People say, "I did that before and my other dog never left the property." Let's face it, you were *lucky*. Do you want to rely on luck? Wouldn't it be smarter to stack the odds in your favor? Aren't you smarter than to stack the odds *against* your beloved pet?

California has a leash law. The law states that if your dog is off leash and off your property, you are automatically in the wrong. Many of us have had a bad experience at some time in our lives due to an aggressive dog suddenly appearing out of nowhere. People on horseback or just walking their dogs, joggers, the newspaper carrier and the mail carrier are all subject to this difficult and dangerous dilemma.

WHAT TO DO WHEN ATTACKED BY A LOOSE DOG

Try to avoid the situation altogether. Do not frequent areas where dogs are known to roam. In the event that an attack is inevitable, **DO NOT RUN!** Running will only cue the dog's prey-chasing drive.

Stand your ground, face the dog and yell "No!" Many dogs have heard this before and will relate it to an aggressive correction. **Do not scream** with a high pitch as this will only excite the dog. Choose a deep tone of voice and show an aggressive posture. Stomp your foot, pick up a rock, anything to out-bully the dog. Fortunately, most dogs that run loose are bullies and will think again.

If this does not work, you must be ready for what comes next. You should already know what you will do if the dog keeps coming at you. If you encounter this problem a lot (because you jog, etc.), dog repellent spray or a stun gun will be helpful in defending yourself. If you do not possess spray or a stun gun, remove a piece of clothing (a rolled-up jacket, shoe, shirt) and feed it to the dog—anything to give you time to back out of the situation. **DO NOT RUN or TURN YOUR BACK** as this will trigger the dog to resume the chase.

If the dog is after your *dog,* be ready for a fight. If the dog actually bites your dog, you have no choice but to allow your dog to fight back. **NEVER get into** the middle of **a dog fight**. The odds are that you will wind up being bitten much worse than either animal. Obviously you do not want your dog to be hurt. You can assist your dog by grabbing the other dog by the tail or the back legs and holding the aggressor dog up *off* the back legs. The aggressor will have no power this way and your dog will have the advantage. If you choose to use this method, you are at risk. The only way to guarantee that you will not be bitten is for you not to participate in the fight.

Personally, with our dogs, we feel that if we expect them to help us survive confrontations with vicious humans, that we should help them to survive attacks by other vicious dogs.

THE RIGHT TO BEAR ARMS

Constitutionally we have the right to own a firearm for our protection, and with that right comes the inherent responsibility to know how to properly handle, use and store that firearm. Of utmost importance is safety. Awareness is an essential part of safety.

Owning a K-9 is also a basic right. However, if you wish to keep that right for yourself and others, safety and awareness are no less important.

DOG HANDLING

Dog handling is different from dog training. Before you learn to train a dog, you must learn basic handling. You are responsible the entire time you have the dog out.

144

Handling Safety Rules

1. Never let two dogs on leashes get closer to one another than 10 feet. (Ten feet is a safe distance if a dog lunges to the end of a 6-foot leash—given a couple of feet or an arm's length—and the possibility of losing your balance.)
2. Do not stand and talk with another person without having your dog under complete control. Be **aware** of what the dog sees. Do not let your dog surprise you by leaping for something and catching you off guard.
3. The dog should be wearing safe and well-fitting equipment. It should be sturdy enough to hold your dog's weight even under pressure.
4. Make sure all doors, gates and latches are kept closed when a dog is put away. Get in the habit of using clasps or locks on latches, thus making them harder to open and harder to forget to close.
5. Do not allow people free access to your dog. People on the street have no business approaching your dog. This only serves to undermine your training. Letting people come up to your dog on the street will only increase your risk of liability.

    You must always respect your dog's abilities even when others fail to. People do some pretty stupid things when meeting a new dog. We have witnessed people who have just met our champion, "Dallas," a 120-pound male Rottweiler, who pull his ears or attempt to look in his mouth. We have to tell them to back off, as Dallas is tolerant but does not take kindly to such presumptuous behavior.
6. Your dog must respect *you*. If you are not "alpha" (leader of the pack), your dog will not listen to you when it is critical. Practice Obedience regularly.

UNDERSTANDING YOUR DOG'S P.O.V. (POINT OF VIEW)

"Tuning in" to your dog's world is a prerequisite to being a good handler. Make a concerted effort to look at the world from the dog's point of view.

Since the wolf is the ancestor of the dog, it helps us to study the wolf in order to better understand our dog. However, dogs have been domesticated for centuries and are therefore not identical to the wolf.

A good handler is always aware of a dog's focus. This photo shows what *not* to do. These handlers are *unaware* of their dogs' focus.

Consider your dog to be a diluted wolf of sorts. This is a result of all of the years of selective breeding that has produced the various breeds we know today.

Instinct

Dogs, like wolves, are highly instinctual creatures. Almost everything wolves do is in order to perpetuate the species. They perceive their world through their senses.

The senses of taste and smell are the most used and the least understood by humans. These senses tell them a variety of things: what they should avoid (i.e., territories to avoid because of scent marking), what is and is not food, where other dogs have been, if a female is in heat, what to avoid because it has a bad smell or taste, and many more.

The last point is important because bad smell or taste can be used to our advantage in training. Scent rolling (the act of rolling in a substance in order to wear the smell) is another form of communication. Another dog will smell the scent wearer. The scent tells the story of where the dog has been. Scent marking and scratching also mark territory and warn others of the dog's presence in the area.

Smell

Scent has been used to our advantage in training for the purpose of tracking lost people and criminals as well as the detection of narcotics and explosives. In all aspects of training, the reward is associated with the find.

The reward can be as mild as a pet from a lost hiker or child to praise from the handler, or in the case of narcotics detection or explosives, a toy is usually the reward. The police dog who has tracked a criminal is rewarded with the possibility of apprehending the criminal.

Dogs recognize their owners primarily by smell. Recognition by sight itself is extremely secondary to recognition by smell. It is no surprise to trainers who demonstrate dogs for hidden owners to find that the dogs will throw their heads up and sniff the air in recognition of the fact that their owners are nearby. It is also not unusual to see a dog cower or growl at the owner on first sight after separation until the owner's scent is recognized.

Hearing

Dogs hear at a rate five to ten times greater than we do. They also have a much greater range of sound where pitch is concerned. This comes in handy when we use them to help protect our homes as they often will hear an intruder long before we do. This ability can cause other problems though. Dogs can also hear the comings and goings of others in the neighborhood and may bark.

Dogs instinctively perceive high tones to mean pleasure and love. On the other hand, low tones mean disapproval and reprimand. Since this is naturally the way that dogs communicate, we can and should use this same system in our communication with them. Humans communicate in much the same way.

It is very difficult to fool a dog. Owners often attempt to sneak up on their dogs in order to "test" their reactions to an intruder. When conditions are just right, this works. However, most often, the dog will have recognized the sound of the car, footsteps or the smell of the owner long before the owner reaches the dog.

Touch

With dogs, touch can be used as an inhibitor as well as a motivator. It should be noted that shock is felt many times greater in intensity to a dog than it is to a human. A dog being petted and at the same time being given a verbal command, will simply *not learn* the command. Dogs are not able to receive more than one kind of input at a time. Since touch is an input, the verbal command is blocked out. You will be wasting time if you pet the dog during a command when training.

This is not to say that tactile praise should not be used in training as it is an effective reward. It is fine as long as it is applied between and after commands. Beyond touch for motivation or inhibition, it can be noted that the basic uses of touch in nature are survival of heat/cold and resistance to pain.

Sight

The ratio of rods to cones in the dog's eye is set up for evening or dawn hours. These are the times when dogs hunt. Dogs are most active at these times of the day even when they do not have to hunt for food. Another natural hunting instinct that dogs possess is that they detect motion at a rate many times greater than ours. This instinct is valuable in protection training.

Dogs do not see with great detail. People recognize faces just as dogs recognize odors. This is why a normally friendly dog may growl if caught off guard. Many people think that a dog can see as well as an owl at night. *This is not true.* However, they can see better than humans because the pupils of their eyes can dilate (open) to a much greater degree than human eyes. Thus, more light is allowed in for greater vision.

YOU AND YOUR DOG AS A TEAM

If you and your dog are to be a dynamic duo, you must first recognize what both of your strengths and weaknesses are. Beyond your own personal quirks and assets on a purely K-9 and human basis, you have a major asset that your dog lacks, that is the ABILITY TO REASON. Because a dog has none, mistakes can be made because canine reactions are based on both instinct and conditioned response.

On the other hand, humans are lacking in instinct by comparison and usually cannot sense changes in sound or scent. If you realize these basics and set out to maximize these assets, you will indeed be a good team.

Knowing your dog's likes, dislikes, fears and weaknesses, as well as the assets will help you to keep the dog safe. For instance, someone jokingly grabbing or pinching you doesn't look much different from someone who is seriously trying to hurt you. Awareness of this will help you both to prevent a negative situation and control the dog by saying everything is "Okay."

PROTECTION TRAINING

The four members of a protection team and their functions are listed below:

1. Dog (minimal age one year) pretrained, tested and ready to go
2. Dog owner/handler, completed basic training
3. Decoy, well-schooled in the art of agitation
4. Training director, calls the shots, observes and directs the action of the K-9 team and decoy

Dog

Before beginning protection training, the dog's ability to get serious is tested. Dogs mature at different rates. You should feel that the dog has mastered committed bites during puppy work. Next, you will test the dog's defense capability. This is where you will see the maturity (or lack of it) in the dog.

Before we begin to explain the defense test, we should explain the art of agitation. There are many misconceptions about how protection dogs are trained. Susan Barwig and Stewart Hilliard, in Chapter 14 of their book *Schutzhund Theory and Training Methods,* put it in simple terms that we would like to repeat here.

> One frequently voiced concern regarding protection is that the training will alter the dog's temperament. However, experience has shown that a dog that is confident and friendly before protection training will remain confident and friendly after protection training. We do not brainwash the animal in any way. We merely strengthen and mold a perfectly natural facet of its behavior that we can already see in some form or degree in the dog before it is ever exposed to agitation.
>
> Another myth surrounding (Schutzhund) bite work is that the training

A novice dog on a defense test may be unsure of himself.

The decoy's backward motion will bring out the dog's courage.

involves cruelty to the dog. Nothing could be further from the truth. After all, the primary objective in bite work is to build and maintain confidence, and this state of being cannot be evoked by cruelty or by force. Confidence and self-assurance evolve instead as a result of a carefully designed series of exercises that teach the dog, first, to display aggression in appropriate circumstances and second, that it can always expect success in so doing. The dog must develop the self-assurance necessary to oppose a human willingly, with conviction and with force. This it will not do if abused or mishandled.

Defense Test

Before entering into protection work a dog must be tested for balance, stability, good nerves and proper drives.

1. Owner/handler stands with dog on a 6-foot leash, attached to a 2-inch police collar.
2. Owner/handler pets and encourages dog for confidence while the decoy sets up behind a blind or bushes some 50 feet away.
3. On "GO," decoy uses a stick or an agitation whip to create noise from the hiding spot so as to rouse the dog's suspicion.
4. As noise begins, handler stops all physical contact and conveys suspicion to the dog. "What's that? Watch 'em!" handler says in an excited tone. Handler watches dog for any sign of alert.
5. Decoy intensifies noise, peeks out of the blind and quickly jumps back as soon as the dog alerts. This builds the dog's confidence and curiosity.
6. Again, any sign of attention or aggression is praised by owner. Owner only pets the dog when agitation subsides.
7. Decoy now begins to be visible moving quickly into and out of the blind, making noise with a stick, hissing and stalking out of and into the blind.
8. Handler must be very enthusiastic and *must participate, not observe*. There must be no correction and unlimited motivation.
9. *Training director* will note the alertness of the dog at a distance to the decoy and decide whether or not to proceed.
10. Next step is to begin to press the dog. The decoy now moves forward and directly challenges the dog, creeping toward the animal, body sideways, so as not to overstress the dog. The

decoy's hand can be outstretched as if to attempt to touch the dog or the owner.

11. Upon the slightest forward movement of the dog, the decoy will quickly pull his or her arm back in and run away like a scared rabbit.
12. This serves to reinforce the defensive action of the dog, who "won" this round.
13. The owner/handler immediately praises the dog for a job well done.
14. The *training director* notes the dog's reaction, and decides if the dog is at a stress peak or can go further.
15. If we proceed to the next step, the decoy now comes up to the safety zone (just out of reach of the dog) and challenges. This encounter is brief. The decoy will run away as the dog shows defense.
16. The owner/handler will again reinforce the dog's behavior with enthusiastic motivation and praise.
17. The dog will be evaluated by the *training director* to assess either a readiness to start or a need for greater maturity.

Dog Handler

It is imperative for a K-9 handler to fully embrace the concept of the safety zone. Most accidents are the result of handler error or equipment failure.

Your primary function as a handler is to control your dog. This involves a lot of holding back while the dog is agitated. When you do so, you must understand that if you are not planted firmly in a good "fighter's" stance, the dog may pull you off balance. If this happens when the decoy is close to the dog, the decoy may be bitten accidentally. The safety zone is the line of demarcation between the dog and decoy at the point where the leash ends. (See diagram.)

Tie Out Lines

One of the reasons tie out lines are frequently used is to avoid these kinds of errors. The tie out is attached to a secure tree or pole. It has a rubber stretch strap attached to absorb the shock of the dog lunging against it. The advantage is obvious, the security zone cannot be breached and the decoy can work unhindered by this possible danger. The time will come when the owner will handle the dog off the line, so this method cannot be used indefinitely.

152

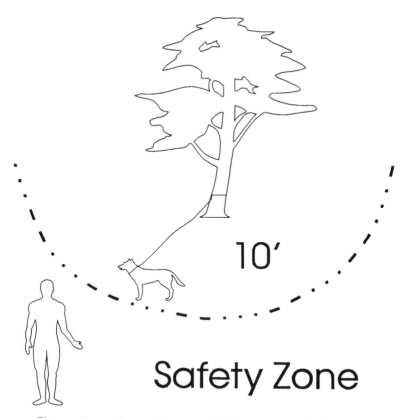

10'

Safety Zone

Diagram shows where safety zone ends. Decoy must stay behind this line.

Holding the Stance

Your stance should be sideways—like you are riding a surfboard. Knees, used to absorb shock, should remain slightly bent. Your center balance should be square so that you move neither forward nor backward.

When our clients attempt this for the first time, we have them hold the leash in both hands as though they were holding the dog. We will give a few yanks on the leash to see if they can hold the stance. It seems to help prepare them for the dog.

Communication with Your Dog

As in Obedience, the beginning phase of protection requires a great deal of communication from you to your dog primarily in the form of cheerleading. If you are nervous, unsure or afraid, you will unintentionally communicate this to the dog and you will both have a very difficult time with this phase of training.

The concept for the handler is to be a cheerleader when the dog is supposed to be uninhibited and displaying all the drives. Soothe, quiet and *control* when the dog is supposed to be on an "Out" (cease agression, see Chapter XIII).

Your Responsibility to the Decoy

Even though this person is your adversary throughout training, you are responsible for protecting the decoy from injury. Often, you (as the handler) will be the only one who can keep a real bite from happening. A dog may go up the arm of a jacket or under the jacket. You must see this and command "Out." If the decoy falls to the ground while being bitten, immediately get yourself between the dog and the decoy's face BEFORE you get the dog off the decoy (see diagram). This is to prevent the dog from going to the face when coming off the bite.

Decoy

The decoy's job is to teach by pushing the dog's prey and defense buttons at the right times. It is an art that takes years to develop. A good decoy knows how to convey a mood or attitude to a dog through body language.

A good decoy also knows how to tell when a dog is going into avoidance (meaning "giving up" with confidence level slipping). The decoy will work the dog to a peak and then put the dog away before getting to the point of avoidance. The good decoy must have a sense for this. It is not something that is taught, it is something that is felt.

Upon seeing avoidance in a dog, a good decoy will make up something to do for the dog to "win" so that the animal can be put away on a high note. Therefore, our new protection prospect should be worked by an experienced decoy. On the other hand, new decoys should work with experienced dogs. In this way, nobody suffers much from mistakes made and everyone benefits from the other's experience.

The Training Director

The training director calls the shots. If he or she is good, the person will not be a dictator but rather will ask for the decoy's and handler's input. Judging by observation and this input, the training

154

director decides when the dog should progress in training or might decide to take a step or two backward temporarily. The training director is generally the most experienced person on staff. This person has been both a handler and decoy previously, and therefore knows how to instruct both parties properly.

Caution to the reader: While most of the materials in this book can be found in print in other trade publications, they are generally published with this warning:

> The novice should not attempt this type of training alone or with another novice. These procedures must be taught under the watchful eye of a licensed professional K-9 trainer.

If you have somehow avoided retaining a professional trainer in the first year of the dog's life, we suggest that you seek one now if you intend to proceed to the protection phase which must be taught carefully and taken very seriously. A novice can—and probably will—ruin the dog for life.

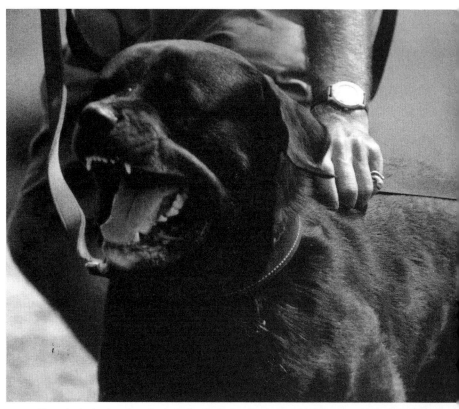

Kingsden's Jawbreaker displays the face of a dog in Level I Protection (threat) Training.

CHAPTER XIII

Level I
Protection Training

CIVIL DEFENSE—THREAT TRAINING

Until this chapter, we have focused on how to prepare the dog for protection training. It is now time to begin to teach the art of K-9 protection.

The dog sport enthusiast who reads this will need to do so with an open mind. While we teach some of the same techniques, we do so from a different perspective and for a different purpose.

Defense is very important to the home protection or Security Patrol K-9. The primary difference in the work is the importance of the equipment. In dog sport, the equipment is of utmost importance. If given the chance, the sport dog will attack the equipment if it is left on the ground. The dog is worked primarily out of the Prey Drive and this attitude reflects this point. There are, of course, sport dogs that are also naturally high in Defense, but in general, it is not a necessity to do well in the sport.

On the other hand, the protection dog is at a loss without a good deal of Defense Drive. The best Schutzhund dogs work at about 60 percent Prey Drive and 40 percent Defense. Conversely, the best protection candidates work at about 60 percent Defense and 40 percent Prey Drive.

Cliff displays Defensive Drive, focusing on the decoy.

Slick displays Prey Drive, focusing on the equipment.

If the percentage of the Prey Drive goes any higher or the Defense Drive any lower, you will have a dog that perhaps looks good on the field, but in real situations will not be naturally defensive enough. In the case of a dog going lower in Prey Drive and higher in Defense, you may have a very good patrol dog, but one you can never fully trust with people. Therefore, sticking to a 60:40 ratio is your best bet.

Commands

The dog can learn any language you wish, as long as it is consistent. Since most people in the U.S. speak either English or German commands (because of German importing throughout the years), we will limit ourselves to the following examples:

Obedience Commands:

English	German
Heel	Fuss
Sit	Sitz
Stay	Bleib
Come	Hier
Down	Platz
No	Pfui
Good dog	Das in fine

Protection Commands:

English	German
Watch 'em	Pass-auf
Speak	Gib laut
Hunt, Check	Revier
Bite	Packen
Hold	Fass
Out	Aus

Equipment Needed

1. 2-inch-wide leather police collar
2. German steel choke
3. 6-foot-long (1-inch wide) police leash with brass clip preferred. Leash can be leather or double-layer nylon.

4. 30-foot-long line (half-inch wide) with brass clip preferred
5. Leather or nylon loop-style tab; 6–10 inches in length
6. Tie out line with rubber connector in center to allow for give
7. Agitation stick or whip—preferably a noisemaker (clatter stick or whip)

Do not allow the dog to eat or drink large amounts of water before or after training. You are better to train a dog with an empty stomach as there is a danger of the stomach twisting (gastric torsion), which can be fatal.

WHAT IS THREAT TRAINING?

Threat training is the process of teaching the dog to act out aggressively to protect his or her house, yard, car and owner. During threat training, we work primarily with the dog's Defensive Drive. The dog's Prey Drive is only used in the sense that as the intruder retreats, the dog gains confidence and wants to give chase.

It is just as important (if not more so) that during this stage of training, we also teach the dog to cease aggression *on command*. This is *unconditional control* on command. The dog must learn that **THE OWNER IS ULTIMATELY IN CONTROL OF ANY AGGRESSION.** Why is the threat process taught before the biting process? There are a number of reasons for this:

1. The dog is learning to be truly aggressive toward the intruder. The dog is not taking cues because of the presence of equipment.

2. Since the dog has had many rewarding hours by now, playfully biting and tugging on the puppy tug, we want to change the attitude from play to true defensiveness. The presence of the puppy tug at this point will only serve to bring back the idea of play.

3. Once the dog's defensiveness is well established, we can begin to teach the "Out," which means to cease aggression. When the owner calls out, the dog should stop barking, growling and lunging. At this point, the dog should sit and behave unless attacked or told otherwise. We have found that teaching the Out in this manner cuts your work in half later on when you teach the dog to Out from the bite.

Can you teach the dog only Level I protection and opt not to progress any further?

YES! Many feel that this is enough training for their needs and will opt not to proceed with bite work. This is acceptable if all that is desired is a cosmetic look of aggression behind a fence or other barrier. If your threat assessment is not high or your dog is not a "hard dog" (one possessing strong nerves and temperament), this may be all you want or can expect from the dog.

However, we must caution that you should not choose this option out of fear of teaching the dog how to bite. If your dog has a solid temperament, teaching how to apprehend someone will not create a dangerous animal. Quite the contrary. If handled properly, bite training will give the dog confidence and teach control. This can be compared to martial arts classes. They do not create bullies, but rather people who have a quiet confidence and who have the ability to act if necessary.

Again, it is important to emphasize that *we must have a well-rounded, stable-minded trio of dog, owner and trainer* to achieve the desired end result.

Won't a well-bred dog be naturally defensive enough?

This is a misconception that many people have. In reality, most people overestimate or underestimate their dog's propensity for aggression. This can lead to accidents or disappointments. A dog left alone to figure out what to do is very likely to do the wrong thing. Police officers have reported that many rapes, burglaries and beatings have taken place with the family Shepherd nearby. The reasons are numerous, not the least of which is the lack of training.

When startled, a dog is faced with two options: fight or flight. If untrained, a dog will make the choice in a split second. Quite frankly, you are just plain lucky if the dog chooses to come to your aid without being taught what to do.

Liability is the other hazard of this way of thinking. The vast majority of accidental dog bites are from untrained dogs. The dogs often are encouraged by their owners to be aggressive until they become neighborhood bullies. The dogs are now fully defensive, but are they controllable?

Dogs demonstrating uncontrolled aggression are a definite liability. We have trained dogs for clients who were at the point that no one would come to visit them because they were afraid of their dogs. The rule of thumb here is that if you rely on your dog as a form of protection, train for it! You will have increased by 70 to 90 percent the chance of your dog acting appropriately when needed.

Are there dogs that will turn on their owners?

There are three factors that can make a dog turn on the owner:

1. Poor or abusive training or handling
2. Poor breeding—dog with low stress level
3. Medical/clinical problem (i.e., brain tumor, psychotic dog)

During training, a dog can be overstressed to the point of becoming uncontrollably defensive. We call this dog a fear biter, one who has learned that defense is the answer to all fears. This dog has a hair trigger, a common result of novice training.

Breeding dogs with poor temperaments can result in dogs with natural fear-biting tendencies. A dog with a low stress level who is taken into protection training will "stress out" and attempt to bite anything available (including the owner). We recommend that this dog never enter a protection program.

Personally, when we run into a dog we feel is dangerous, we write a statement of our findings and have the owner sign it. We recommend that such a dog be kept in a secure dog run unless under the owner's immediate supervision or on a leash. In extreme cases, we have had to recommend that certain dogs be put to sleep because of their viciousness. This happens most often when an owner of a two- to four-year-old dog with no training brings the animal to us and says, "Can you fix him?"

If you follow the program we have laid out for you in this book, this is a problem you will not encounter.

THREAT TRAINING

The safety collar is an extra collar attached to the tie out just in case the first collar breaks. Judging by the aggressiveness and strength of the dog, you may even utilize a second safety line.

Focus on the Intruder/Attacker

Step 1 Goal: Teach the dog to be alert and bark on command.

Wearing a two-inch leather collar, the dog should be anchored to the tie out line. The safety collar (large choke collar) should also be loosely attached. The dog is held by the handler at the end of the line in the Heel position. The dog does not have to sit or perform any Obedience tasks.

On "Go," the agitator approaches in a manner consistent with the temperament of the dog (i.e., at a distance for a weak civil dog, closer for a strong civil dog). The decoy moves in a quick jerky motion to attract the dog's attention. To the dog, the decoy seems to appear aggressive and fearful at the same time. A skilled decoy knows how to seemingly challenge one moment and to jump back fearfully the next with body language.

With the first sign of aggression or forward movement (on the part of the dog), the decoy pulls in and runs for the hills. The handler verbally lavishes praise on the dog when the decoy is present and then physically when the decoy is out of sight. This builds the dog's confidence and quickly teaches the dog to relieve the stress of the situation with forward motion, a bark or growl.

Timing is critical when teaching the dog the meaning of the commands. When the decoy first appears, you should tell your dog to be alert by saying "On Guard" or "Pass-auf" (German). Your dog will begin to look for trouble in association with your warning.

Some breeds are much more natural than others when it comes to barking. German Shepherd Dogs, for instance, are much more likely to bark quickly than Rottweilers. The command for bark is "Gib laut" (German). We say "Watch 'em" (English). These are typical commands; however, you can use anything you like.

Step 2 Goal: Teach the dog to cease aggression on command.

Once the dog will alert on command and bark on command, we will need to teach "Out" (English) or "Aus" (German). This means to cease aggression and behave. We command the dog to "Out" and to "Sit."

This step may need to be initiated as early as the third day of threat training for a hard (aggressive) dog, and possibly as late as three weeks for a soft (less aggressive) dog. This time, the dog also wears a training collar, a steel choke—typically the same type used for

Using the tie-out line the dog can lunge against the line without undo shock to his neck (note rubber strap). On "Out", the dog should sit quietly as the decoy passes by.

Obedience. This is worn around the throat above the police collar. The 6-foot line is attached to the training collar. The line is not held tight, as you must be careful *not to correct* when the dog is on the alert or bark command.

On cue, the decoy will cease agitation. You should command the dog to "Out." From this point on, when aggressive, the dog is corrected with "No" and a jerk which should be remembered from Obedience.

Next, give the command "Sit" and praise. At this point, pet the dog on the head or scratch behind the ear. As the dog is soothed and remains calm, repeat "Out, Good Out." The decoy should be able to casually walk by, back and forth as the handler keeps the dog under control.

Step 3 Goal: Teach the dog to trust your judgment.

Now that the dog understands the concept of alert, bark and out, it is important to teach the trust of your judgment and your commands. The dog now understands being aggressive toward other aggressive behavior and being calm on "Out" when things calm down. The question becomes, what if there is a need to be aggressive when things seem calm, or calm when things seem aggressive? The only way for you to ensure this behavior is to proceed to the next two steps, "friendly agitation" and "agitating outs."

Friendly Agitation

Friendly agitation involves teaching the dog to trust your judgment and not to trust anyone else. Throughout their lives, most dogs have learned that a friendly acting person is a friendly person. This can work against you if your assailant decides not to speak loudly or to move quickly. It is possible to be threatened with a weapon or verbally assaulted without the gestures that might cue your dog. It is not unusual for the potential stalker to assess your dog and try to sweet-talk or get past the animal with a tidbit. This is why it is so important to teach the dog that your judgment is all that matters. *Remember, dogs do not have the ability to reason. Therefore, legally it is important that the dog listens to you unconditionally.*

Using both police and training collars, the dog (again on the tree) is approached by the decoy. The first agitation will be typical aggressive agitation followed by an "Out" for control.

Next, the decoy will approach in a friendly manner, sweet-talk and pat his or her knee with hand extended as if to offer the dog a treat. During this time, the handler gives the dog *aggressive cues* ("Pass-auf" and "Gib laut"). Typically, the dog will fall for it at least one time. The dog will be confused but will most likely cave in to the longest term conditioning which is to trust.

The handler then tells the dog "No," "Pass-auf," "Gib laut." At this point, the decoy will show true intentions and will tap the dog on the nose or ear and then jump back. The dog will quickly realize the handler was right and that he (the dog) has been suckered.

Repeat this process until the dog no longer buys into the sucker routine. Do not be surprised at first if the dog tends to be more aggressive on friendly agitation as this is a typical reaction to a loss of innocence.

Step 4 Goal: Teaching Agitating Outs

Now that we have taught the dog to listen to your judgment in what seems to be a friendly situation, we will throw the dog another curve by teaching that all seemingly aggressive acts are not necessarily what they appear to be.

The decoy will approach the dog, who is once again on the line and wearing both collars. The dog is commanded to "Out" and is soothed. The decoy jogs by at a rapid pace, sparking the dog's Prey Drive. The decoy then may turn quickly and with raised arms. Your decoy has the option to approach the dog and scamper away, reach to pet the dog and quickly pull back or yell, scream and hit a bush with the stick, just about anything except for directing aggression toward the dog.

All of this time, the handler of the dog should be controlling the dog with command "Out" and praise "Good dog," "Good Out" and the strong controlled correction "No" anytime the dog presumes to make an independent judgment.

Step 5 Goal: Holding the Dog Back—The Handler in Control

Once all of the steps are followed and the dog is listening properly to all cues, you are ready to remove the tie out line.

Now the handler is responsible for holding the dog back. Before giving the handler this responsibility, it is best to talk the handler through proper stance. The training director should give the person the leash and request that it be held as if the dog was on the end of it. Grab the leash and give it a yank equal to what the dog might give. The handler should remain planted. This person should be taught to center themselves if they move forward and to absorb the shock without moving.

The dog should now wear the police collar held by the police leash. The training collar should have a 10-inch tab connected to it and the leash should be run through the loop of the tab to the protection collar. The other option is the police circular leash with a clasp on each end. As the handler assumes control of the dog physically, you will run systematically through all of the steps.

NOTE: All *agitation sessions* should be *short* as your dog expends a great deal of energy during this process. There is a lot of mental stress on the dog as well. It is not unusual to work a dog on each series only three to six times. You can negate your training by overworking or overstressing the dog.

Some critics may think it unnecessary to teach the dog not to trust. Our argument for this is based on simple reality. These dogs are expected to face real life situations. The majority of human beings learn sometime in their adult lives not to trust strangers. It is only natural to teach a protection dog not to trust strangers no matter what the ploy.

For protection work the options are: the leash put through the tab; or the circular police leash with clasps on both ends.

BOUNCING BOUVIERS AND OTHER BREEDS

Some breeds, such as Bouviers, have a tendency to jump straight up in the air when they are agitated. The danger is in the dog falling backward onto its spine or coming down wrong on a leg. To prevent this, the handler must hold the leash down by the collar and lock elbows so as to hold the dog down. The decoy can also help by agitating in a lower manner, rather than up toward the dog's head.

SITUATION SETUPS

We are appalled by the number of trainers who claim that they train dogs for home protection, yet do not offer to go to the home to train the dog.

Dogs are conditioned creatures. To learn techniques in protection is great; however, the result is the dog gets a "field mentality." In the dog's mind, protection takes place only when in the field. This associates being home with being on "vacation."

We have worked with police department dogs and Schutzhund

167

In threat training the dog is agitated without use of equipment for realism.

IIIs with many years of experience who were caught off guard when the intruder showed up at home. The dogs' general response is, "Hey, we don't do this here!" However, it does not take these dogs long to adjust. The message is loud and clear. If home is where one is supposed to work, then doesn't it seem to follow that the dog should be taught to work in the home?

There are four areas we generally work the dogs in:

- House
- Yard
- Car
- With the owner

AGITATING AT THE HOME

Prior to coming to the home for the first time, the decoy should preplan with the handler exactly what will be done and how it will be handled. There is no time in the heat of battle to stop and discuss things. The idea here is to create as realistic a situation as possible.

The first encounter will be the hardest for the dog. Plan to make it easy and not work the "Out" on this lesson. This can be adjusted in case the dog needs to work on control. With the advent of car phones, we now have it easier. We can talk to the client without the dog having the slightest idea what is taking place. We generally have the dog lying in the Place command when we begin. Make sure that the handler holds the dog back well enough that the dog does not knock things over, scratch the doors or go through the windows.

Naturally, the dog is generally the most confident when in home territory. Behind a door, window or gate, the dog is safe from harm and knows it. Allow this advantage during the first lesson by agitating in these areas only. Keep in mind that the decoy's retreat is important in building confidence.

With each lesson, we will expand the training a bit further. We will put the dog in the car and teach car protection with and without the owner present. We will work on handler protection as the handler walks down the street or to the ATM. The dog will learn to check the house for intruders and warn the owner by barking if someone is hiding out.

To maintain balance, we must practice control as well. Intermittently, we will set up a passive situation such as playing the role of salesperson. The dog can be alert, but must not be aggressive unless commanded to become so.

CHECK COMMAND

Purpose: To teach the dog to check the house for intruders and to warn the owner of people hiding there.

Prior to teaching this command, we should have worked on all of the other avenues of civil defense around the house and neighborhood.

We will now go out to the front yard facing the house and hold the dog with the usual equipment (police and training collars) setup. The decoy approaches from the front of the house and agitates the dog. When the dog is sufficiently worked up, the decoy runs into the house and hides in a predesignated place.

After giving the decoy sufficient time to hide, the handler takes the dog into the house and gives the command to "Check." In the beginning, we will intersperse this command with "Watch 'em, Check," since the Check command is new and we want the dog to remain on track.

When you enter the house, the determining factor of how quickly the dog finds the intruder will be how natural it is for the dog to use the sense of scent. Other people should not be in the house as a serious accident could result if someone startles the dog. The animal should be intent on looking for the intruder. The first find should be fairly easy and set up.

Upon entering the house, you should be cognizant of two factors: air circulation and quartering the area.

Air Circulation

It will be much more difficult for your dog to find the intruder if the air conditioning is on, because the air will be circulating the scent in various directions. Turn off all fans and do not have food cooking as this is very distracting to a dog.

Quartering the Area

Even though this is a training setup, we must teach the handler proper procedures in case of a real life situation. When entering the home, each room has to be cleared systematically before moving on. This is important so the intruder does not end up behind you.

Pay close attention to the dog's cues. After you have practiced with this dog many times, you will begin to understand the dog's indications. Typically, a dog will become excited and begin to pull into the leash, with tail up and head down in order to scent.

Do not pull your dog away from the scent. Use trust!

In most cases, if you believe someone is in your home, you should leave and call the police. It is extremely dangerous for both you and your dog to go in.

You must remember that a protection dog is meant to be used **DEFENSIVELY,** *not* **OFFENSIVELY!** Even a police K-9 unit uses caution when sending a K-9 in after a hidden suspect, because there is no way of knowing if this person is armed.

We have trained a number of personal K-9s for police officers and their families as well as security personnel. These people are usually armed and better trained for such situations. Extreme caution is still advised.

It is wise to announce at the door that the intruder should come out or the K-9 will be sent in. Do not do this unless you are armed and prepared if the intruder comes out shooting. Your best bet is to back off and call the police.

If the dog is allowed to check the house and locates the intruder, the dog should give a strong indication that the person is hidden behind the door or wherever. During this portion of *training,* the handler pulls the dog back and the decoy comes out agitating the dog. When the dog's aggression peaks, the decoy turns and runs. The handler and the dog give chase, stopping at the doorway.

You must be very careful to give the decoy a good head start. While training is taking place inside, doors should remain open for easy escape. This is very scary for the decoy. Even if 20 feet behind, it feels as if the dog is right on top of the decoy.

We feel it is important to point out that in order to provide protection for you, the dog needs to be with you. This is one reason that we concentrate so much on obedience and manners. The easier the dog is to live with, the more likely that you will have your dog with you.

GETTING PAST THE DOG

Our experience in real life encounters with the bad elements of society points out certain typical procedures they employ. Most stalkers assess their target's vulnerability prior to attacking. This is why you want a potential stalker to see that the dog is with you. This alone will force a stalker to think twice about choosing you as a target.

Try not to be predictable as to when you leave the dog outside or in your home. The more time and effort necessary to get at you, the less likely a stalker is to bother you.

The following is a case in point. At one time, we had a client who called us after being raped in her own home. She was a widow who lived alone in a beautiful home in a nice neighborhood in Orange County, California. She was not too concerned about her safety in general because she lived in a nice area, a common misconception. She had purchased a German Shepherd Dog because of the night stalker who had been on the loose the previous year in Southern California. Following the night stalker's subsequent capture, her fears subsided and she chose not to follow through with the dog's training. What she did not know was that she was being watched and the stalker knew that her dog was left outside at night.

One fateful night, the woman was awakened by the dog's frantic barking. She guessed (incorrectly) that the dog was responding to a cat on the fence and promptly fell back asleep. In actuality, the dog was responding to someone who had opened the garage door and who was attempting to gain access into her home.

She was startled awake by a hand covering her mouth. The man was on top of her. She fought him and managed to bolt downstairs.

Her single thought was to let the dog in the house. The dog was now lunging at the back door. Although untrained, the dog was desperately trying to help the owner. Unfortunately, she was caught by the man a mere 15 feet from the door. She was raped, beaten and robbed 15 feet from her dog. She was fortunate to survive this ordeal.

Since then the dog has been trained for protection and now sleeps next to her at night. If the dog had been previously left inside, the stalker most likely would have gone elsewhere. In any case, the stalker would have had to go through the dog to get to her. At the very least, she would have had a chance. As the saying goes, "An ounce of prevention is worth a pound of cure."

WHY CIVIL DEFENSE BEFORE BITE WORK?

The idea of biting has been preconditioned into the dog. If we fail to instill this idea at an early age, the dog will more easily be put into avoidance, as most families unconsciously squelch the drives of the dog by correcting all forms of growling, barking and biting and installing discipline with Obedience. Too much of this can squelch both the Prey and Defense Drives to the point that the dog will *avoid* any direct aggressive encounter with a human.

There are many different theories regarding this. A common viewpoint is that the dog should not experience any discipline in the first year of life. Those who advocate this point of view claim that a dog will have full use of natural Defense and Prey Drives if they have not been squelched by compulsive Obedience.

We have found there are two basic flaws to this theory:

1. *If you wait until the dog is physically and emotionally mature before applying discipline, you have lost the imprint and conditioning periods.* Therefore, you create a narcissist who needs to be disciplined with compulsion. The truth to this statement can be seen in many dogs involved in European sport who are disciplined with the use of shock collars or prong collars. The trainers are not doing this to be cruel, but rather as a necessity to gain control over a dog who has never known discipline. We would rather see the dog worked in both Obedience and preprotection at a level appropriate to the age of the dog.
2. An obvious drawback to the "no Obedience theory" is that it is downright impossible to live with a dog that you cannot discipline. In order to be a member of the family, the dog must learn to behave in the house, yard, car, etc.

Many European sport enthusiasts keep their dogs in kennels unless they are working with them. This is the only way you can tolerate an undisciplined dog, so if the dog is only used for sport and/or breeding purposes, this may not be a problem.

However, this book deals with the companion-protection dog. The word companion means that the dog spends time with you. We have spoken with many European trainers for sport dogs who freely admit that if they leave their dogs alone in the house or yard, they are likely to return to a disaster. Many of them accept this as part of the price paid for living with a dog that has been raised for sport.

In no way do we wish to suggest that these trainers are wrong. It is purely their choice of how they want to train dogs for their purposes. It is also their choice as to what they are willing to tolerate in their everyday lives.

In order to be effective, the companion-protection dog must be "livable" enough to be with you. Thus, we feel the best compromise is a balance of discipline using mild compulsion and drive work in the first year of life.

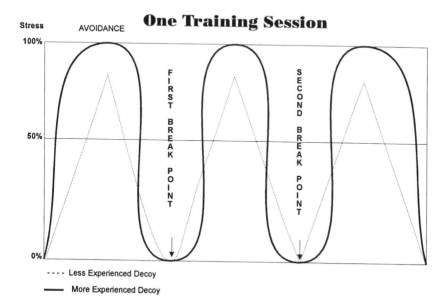

This graph represents the dog's learning curves. The top of the curve is the avoidance point. Professional trainers can work the dog right up to the peak of this curve. Less experienced trainers should not work so near to the point of avoidance. Working up to 75% of the dogs stress peak is safer than chancing putting the dog into avoidance.

LEARNING CURVES

It is important to understand that in protection training, the dog will go through peaks and valleys in training. It is not unusual for a dog to be excellent one day and terrible the next. This is why the decoy's and training director's roles are so vital. They must decide when to go forward and when to back off. For both physical and psychological reasons, dogs are ever-changing creatures and must be evaluated from day to day.

The best trainers will instinctively know how far they can take dogs before pushing them into avoidance. A dog will need to be monitored carefully until settled into training, a point requiring a minimum of two years' time.

The period of time between one and two years of age is the most volatile for a young dog, who is just becoming an individual and figuring out what to do with natural drives. This is why it is so important to stabilize aggression early.

CHAPTER XIV

Level II
Protection Training
(6–30-Foot Line)

UP TO THIS POINT, we have not used equipment in our agitation. This is because we want to fix the dog's mind firmly on the decoy intruder or agitator. Equipment would distract from this process. Now, due to necessity, we must return to the use of equipment.

Equipment to be used:

1. Full-body police bite suit of European design
2. German sleeves—puppy, intermediate and advanced
3. Agitation sticks—bamboo, whip and reed
4. Tie out line
5. Collars—training collars, 2-inch police collar
6. Leashes—6-foot police leash, 30-foot-long line

The next question is going to be the style of training for the dog. This will be determined by the desires of the owner and the job description of the dog.

People who also desire to work their dogs for a Schutzhund degree, breed suitability test or protection tournament, may want to stick with the use of the German sleeve. After the desired goals are

Biting boldly. The sleeve is an alternate piece of equipment used to teach a dog to bite with a full mouth.

achieved in this area, conversion training for realism using the European police suit may follow.

For the person who is solely realism-minded, the police suit is the only way to go. We prefer to teach the dog on the legs first and then switch to upper torso and body bites. Some of the softer home protection dogs may have difficulty with the legs. If this gets to be a hindrance to your training, it is our experience that it is best to teach upper torso bites rather than put the dog into avoidance.

Remember that unlike Schutzhund, police, military and security K-9s, the home protection dog is not always a perfect candidate. Many people desire to give their dogs whatever training possible, even if the dog shows limited ability. The personal protection trainer must, therefore, be very flexible in the level and style of training. It is essential for the trainer to be up-front with the client regarding a dog's capabilities. If the dog is balanced enough for training, but limited in the areas of courage, drives or nerves, the client must be informed enough to make an educated decision whether or not to proceed with this dog in training.

ON-LEASH APPREHENSION WORK

Step 1: Teaching the Bite—Slipping Equipment

By this time, you should have had plenty of experience teaching the dog biting and head turning with the puppy tug. If you have somehow missed this step, you will need to cover it here before you move on.

The next move will be to introduce the biting equipment which will be the pants, the jacket or the sleeve, depending upon the dog and your purpose. In any case, your goal is to teach the dog to bite the equipment and bite it powerfully. In order to do this, we must switch the focus of attention from the Defensive Drive to the Prey Drive. To accomplish this, we will attempt to separate the equipment from the person temporarily.

We take the equipment and swing it in front of the dog in a teasing fashion. The dog is finally rewarded with the equipment after a short tug-of-war, and should then be allowed to carry the equipment away.

This can (and should) be done with both the tie out line *and* the handler holding the leash. Both of these have advantages and disadvantages. The tie out makes it easier for the decoy to work safely and to create a better bite by stretching the dog on the line. The handler

To begin to teach the dog leg bites we must teach him to turn his head to the side while biting.

The dog's head should be turned from side to side without over turning.

Next the dog learns to turn his own head to grab the vertical tug.

The pants are introduced only after the dog will rotate his head to bite. The decoy is held so that he cannot be pulled into the dog.

holding the leash helps to improve confidence by allowing the dog to carry the prey (equipment) away.

Step 2: Teaching Out and Guard

You will put the equipment on only after you feel the dog is committed to the equipment. You do not want the dog to concentrate on your face or your hands as if in a defensive mode. You want your dog looking straight at the target area on the equipment.

To do this, the decoy must ensure that the target is moving and is the most obvious thing about the decoy. The target must move horizontally across the dog's plane of vision. *If it is the arm,* we swing it in a sideways motion across the body and in front of the dog's field of view. *If it is a leg* we are using, we must kick out to the side offering the leg just below the knee to the dog. This looks like a martial arts side kick or a soccer kick.

It is very important that the handler hold the dog down on all fours when teaching leg bites. Locking your elbow with your hand close to the collar will prevent the dog from being able to go up high on the decoy. To concentrate on the legs, the decoy cannot wear the jacket and, therefore, this technique is very important for safety.

Once the dog has a good hold, the decoy must keep the prey (equipment) moving in order to keep the dog focused. When the decoy stops fighting, the handler grabs the dog's collar and holds the dog up off the front paws. The dog lets go when the handler commands "Out," causing the dog to release the bite. At this point, the handler sits the dog down right in front of the decoy and while holding the dog in position, tells the dog to guard the decoy. When the decoy attempts to get away, the handler gives the command to bite again and the dog is given the equipment as a reward. If the decoy cannot slip the pants, you must give the "Out" command to the dog and have the decoy jump out of reach.

Step 3: Bite, Out, Guard and Reattack

In this step, the dog comes off the tie out and is held by the handler. The dog who has learned on the legs up until now must be taught an extra step—that is to bite the jacket as well. When the dog comes off the tie out, it is important for the decoy's safety to wear the jacket. For the first time, the team will practice the basic series in protection: **Bite, Out.**

180

Teaching beginning bite work requires the tie out line to hold the dog in place. The decoy can then apply the proper amount of resistance.

At the proper time the decoy rewards the dog with the equipment and runs away, acting afraid in order to build the dog's confidence.

Teaching the dog to "let go" on "Out" is best taught from behind the decoy. This type of correction will not hurt the dogs mouth (Note the position of handler).

Guard and Reattack

Holding the dog the handler waits for the decoy to work the dog up and come for the bite. The decoy fights with the dog and then freezes. On cue from the decoy, the handler gives the "Out" command and asks the dog to sit and guard. If there is difficulty with the Out, the handler corrects the dog forward *into the bite, not away* from it. This is to protect the dog's teeth from harm.

The handler sits the dog in front of the decoy with the "Guard" command. When the decoy makes a move, the dog will reattack. At first you can help with a bite word—"Packen," or "Fass." However, later you will not have to. The dog must be cheered and praised for every correct action.

Following the reattack, the dog may be given the equipment. However this time, after the dog's brief enjoyment of the reward, the decoy will return threatening the dog. The handler will bring the dog back on the decoy *rather than the equipment*. The timing of this move is very important and should not be done at all if the dog is biting softly.

Step 4: 6-Foot Leash—Basic Series and Transport

The dog is now familiar with the entire series of moves. We must teach not to anticipate that there will always be just one attempted escape. We will begin to have the dog defend against one to three escapes at random. This way, a dog knows never to stop watching the decoy until the handler gives a command to come away or go to the Heel position.

The escapes can happen at any time. They can occur just after the dog releases the bite, during the handler's search of the decoy for weapons or during the transport. Once the dog learns this, it will not be taken for granted that the decoy is passive once being stopped by the dog.

To practice this, the handler will send the dog on the bite to the end of a 6-foot line and will then command the dog to "Out" and guard. Here the decoy has the option to attempt to escape. The handler will then proceed to leave the dog's side after telling the decoy to raise his or her hands.

At this point, many handlers prefer to put the dog on a Down and guard. It helps to ensure holding the position and gives the decoy valuable seconds to bring his or her arms down if the dog springs. This is a time when the decoy's stomach can be vulnerable if the dog goes under the jacket.

The handler steps behind the decoy and takes the stick. At this time, the decoy can attempt an escape. The handler then returns to the dog, gives a command to Heel and takes the dog to the decoy's right Heel position. Now the dog is between the handler and decoy. The handler now commands the decoy to walk forward. As they walk together in a line, the dog should be aware that the decoy can make a break for it. If this happens the dog must reattack. The decoy is transported to the training director and the exercise is complete.

Step 5: 30-Foot-Long Line Series and Transport

The next step is practicing the same series with random escapes but with the dog working up to a 30-foot distance. This is the step that will separate the mediocre dogs from the truly courageous animals. The only thing that is different here from all previous work is that you are no longer fighting side by side with your dog. Now you are sending the dog to fight alone with only your verbal encouragement from the rear.

Leg bites should not be taught by a novice. It can be dangerous work. The dog must first target the proper area.

The kick must be presented at just the right time. The dog must be held down by the handler.

Working on the long line bridges the gap between on- and off-leash. This allows the dog to build momentum for the bite.

The dog learns to guard the man after the apprehension. The dog will not let the decoy move unless the handler calls the dog away.

To some dogs, this makes no difference whatsoever. With others, this is a devastating turn of events. If your dog has difficulty with distance, work slowly and gradually increase the distance. You can still work off-leash, but what you are seeing is a lack of self-confidence. This generally will not happen if the dog is genetically well-bred for working, has a good relationship with the owner and has had sound training.

CHECK COMMAND—THE BARK AND HOLD

Now that we have taught the dog how to bite, we must teach a second command just to hold someone. We use the English word "Check." You may also use "Search," "Find," "Revier" (German), etc. This word should mean locate, bark and hold to the dog unless the person moves.

Step 1: Decoy Comes to Dog

As with any other command, we must first show the dog what we want. In order to do this, the decoy approaches the dog slowly and methodically. The dog should be encouraged to bark and carry on, but at the same time the handler should hold the dog short and praise. The decoy eventually should be within reach of the dog, but as the decoy is not moving, the dog maintains a bark and hold. After the dog gives several intense barks, the dog is rewarded with the bite.

Step 2: Handler and Dog Go to Decoy with 6-Foot Leash

After the dog knows the Check command (meaning only to bark at the decoy until he or she moves), you are ready to take the dog to the decoy. You execute basically the same thing in reverse as in Step 1. This time you give the command and you proceed slowly (although the dog will be quicker than the decoy in Step 1) to the decoy and encourage the dog to bark and hold. Again, when the decoy moves, the dog is rewarded with a bite.

Step 3: Bark and Hold on 30-Foot Line

Now that the dog has the idea firmly ingrained that "Check" means to go to the decoy and bark and hold, you are ready to let the dog go faster and without you close behind.

186

Starting 15 feet away from the decoy, send the dog on a Check command. Just as the dog gets to the decoy, tighten the leash so that a bite is *not* possible. Encourage and calm your dog at the same time. You may need to control, pet and soothe the dog. You may have to tell the dog to "Gib laut" or whatever bark command you use. The dog must bark six to twelve times before getting rewarded by being able to bite.

SITUATION SETUPS

Now that all of your field work is accomplished, we must move to the situation work. Again, setups are important to ensure that your dog will respond properly if and when necessary. The dog must learn to carry out the tasks learned:

- In the house
- In the yard
- In the car
- While walking with the handler

In the House

The first setups again will be at doors, windows and gates. The decoy will practice setting the dog up so as to add surprise to the scenario.

The basic bite-out guard and transport should be practiced. Next the decoy will escalate attacks by forcing entry into the home. In all cases, we will also include nonaggressive scenarios so that the dog does not think that every time someone comes to the door, it is someone bad.

The same thing goes for the yard. The dog learns not to let anyone come into the yard without the owner present. The decoy can also practice fleeing from the house through the backyard, or you can have the dog sent on the decoy from the house.

Check the House

The check of the house is handled in the same way as Level I, except this time the decoy wears the suit to be able to take the bite. Keep in mind that this time the dog associates the words "Check" or "Search" with checking the house *and* with the bark and hold. Now

Canto finds the man hiding in the closet on the Check command.

the decoy does not have to be behind a barrier, and can be around a corner. Your decoy is well-protected because of the suit.

The dog is now worked much the same as previously with one basic difference—there is now a direct confrontation with the intruder/decoy. Once the decoy moves, the dog is free to bite and apprehend. The search and transport should be carried out now.

STREET WORK

We now need to expand training to go outside of the neighborhood. Dog and handler should meet the decoy at a predesignated location and time. A bank ATM machine is a good choice of location.

Set up an actual mock assault using the whole series as a routine. Next put the dog in the car with the owner handling. You may do a bite setup in the car. Make sure the window is halfway down to allow for the dog's head and the decoy's arm. "Outs" have to be quick as the dog will often back up, pulling the decoy into the car.

CAUTION: Always work your dog on leash in a public area, even when the dog is in the car. *Be aware of whether or not you are causing a scene.* We have a sign that we put out that says, "Dog training in progress." You never know when someone will panic and call the police because they do not know what is going on.

Also, in situation setups in the home, you must notify the neighbors before the trainer begins this part of the training. People tend to overreact and jump to conclusions. We have had some close calls and have almost been shot at before because a neighbor thought a real robbery was in progress.

STICK WORK

Stick work in Level II protection should be light and should mainly consist of noise, petting and patting. Because we are developing the dog's techniques we do not want to overstress or put the dog into avoidance now. There will be plenty of time for building up intensity in the next two phases of protection training.

Nana comes roaring into the blind on a search.

CHAPTER XV

Level III Protection Training— Off-Leash Protection

BODY BITES AND FALL DOWNS

NOW THAT THE DOG has learned the basics of personal protection, we can intensify training. Your dog has been in serious protection training for four to six months by now and should be reasonably self-confident. We are now ready to teach a more advanced style that will involve teaching body bites, transfers, stick hits, kicks, obstacle and noise distractions.

Step 1: On-Leash Body Bites and Fall Downs

This phase of training teaches the dog how versatile a dog can be when it comes to where the bite is given. It is now up to the decoy to present different body biting areas for the dog. The shoulder can be given by a simple half turn at the correct time. The exposed body part is the shoulder. Since the shoulder is up high, once the dog bites, he or she should be picked up and then set down to recover strength, after

It is critically important that the handler is in place between the decoy's head and the dog *before* calling the dog off the bite when the decoy is down.

which the dog can be picked up again. Practice should also take place on the inside of the arms, the stomach, the back, the back of the legs and the rear end of the decoy.

It is now time to add some realism into the sounds of protection work. The decoy should begin to scream and yell. The dog can be taught that if hit properly, the decoy will fall to the ground—an excellent confidence builder for the dog. It is essential that when the decoy goes down, the handler protects the decoy's face. This is accomplished by putting the handler between the dog and the decoy's face before calling the dog off. One should *never* call the dog off a decoy on the ground before the handler has control of the dog. The chance of the dog going into the decoy's face is very high if the handler is not right there to control the situation.

Step 2: Long Line Preparations for Off-Leash Bites

As previously stated, the long line work will display the true working qualities of the dog. A truly hard dog will not have any problem with the presence of the long line. On the other hand, the soft

The double long line technique allows the handler's hands to be free while progressing the dog toward off-leash work.

dog may balk at it and may hesitate to drag the line or leave your side. You will have to eliminate the line for this dog and work on the light line or off-leash at this point. It will not matter much because this dog is generally very obedient and controlled on the Outs. Building this dog's intensity and confidence is the problem. Therefore, you will need to do a lot of run away work with this kind of dog.

A more common problem is that the dog does not "feel" the Out (letting go) until the handler is right there. There are generally three ways of correcting the dog's way of thinking:

- Handler correction, with long line
- Training director correction, with long line
- Decoy correction, with leash

Step 3: Light Line Work with Stick Hits and Distractions

The dog is now ready to progress to the light line or Toy breed leash. By this time, the dog should be solid on all commands. However, the line is here just in case we need to apply a correction.

The decoy begins by putting more pressure on the dog in the form of stick hits and kicks. *A good decoy knows how to do this without hurting the dog.* The dog is **NEVER** hit on the head, and is only struck

193

If the dog has trouble with leg bites off leash . . .

he can be put on the leg. The handler can then let go and issue verbal commands.

194

on the sides or on the thick muscles of the back. Because the sticks are made of lightweight reed and bamboo materials, and because of the dog's thick coat the animal is not harmed in any way. As for kicks, they are only of *minimum strength* with the side of the foot. Our intention is to teach the dog what may be encountered, *not to discourage*. **Hurting the dog would defeat the purpose.**

It is time to become creative. The decoy may choose to block the dog's path with various articles, bang trash cans, topple chairs, throw wads of paper at the dog, throw a cup of water or play matador and miss when the dog comes in for a bite. A certain amount of this is good for the dog. It is up to the experienced decoy and training director to know when the dog has had enough.

Step 4: Off-Leash Situations

Now is the time to take off the leash and only have the tab on the collar just in case you need the control. If the dog still shows an occasional lack of willingness to Out, the handler may want to knot a choke chain and use it as a throw chain at the dog's hindquarters. Sometimes it works to have a third party do this so the dog can never be sure where the correction will come from. Now you can have some fun with various situations.

Put the dog on a Down Stay and wait for your dog to settle down. Meet the decoy in the center of the field and shake hands. Correct if the dog breaks.

Next, the decoy should stroll away. Turn your back to the decoy. Now have the decoy sneak up on you and grab you from the back. Your dog should immediately come to your aid. If the dog hesitates, command the dog on what to do. Be careful that you are not positioned between the dog and decoy, as you could accidentally be bitten. The decoy should always be between the dog and you, and should push you away when the dog bites the decoy.

Attack Out of Bushes or Blind

Take a walk with your dog. Have the decoy hide in a predesignated spot. As you approach, the decoy should jump out at you. The dog should perform the basic routine. The decoy can decide what number of escapes to attempt.

After a dog is confident in bite work, making him miss adds a degree of realism.

The dog must change focus to whatever is available. In this case the decoy's rear end.

After he is called "Out" Dallas backs away far enough to keep a good watch on the man.

Nana executes a bark and hold after finding the man.

Step 5: Call Offs (only for hard dogs)

A call off is when you send a dog on a bite and at the last second you command to ''Out.'' The dog must not bite. Many hard dogs require this exercise. It is easily practiced with a long line. Whether you correct with the line (or someone else does), the timing is critical. The dog should immediately be called back to the Heel position.

If you have been experiencing difficulties in getting the dog to bite with sufficient intensity, *do not try this exercise*. Such a dog would fold and refuse to bite the next time sent. This dog would be called off easily anyway. Control is not the problem here.

BARK AND HOLD OFF LEASH

Now that the dog has learned to "Search" or to "Check," both on the field and in the home, we will advance in both areas to the off-leash search.

STEP 1

Set up a place for the decoy to hide. A training blind is best, as it is portable and you can place it anywhere you like. Bushes and trees are the next best alternative. Have the decoy make noise and send the dog in on a search. You may have the training director in place, so that if the dog takes a cheap bite, you can give a correction with the throw chain.

STEP 2

Now we change things on the dog by hiding the decoy in a different blind. On command to search, the dog will run to the blind where the decoy usually hides. If the dog comes up empty, reissue the command. It is acceptable if the decoy needs to make noise in the blind to help the dog the first time.

All of your basic Bite-Out-Guard, Reattack and Escorts remain the same. Adjustments are made for the sake of control or confidence as you go along.

IN-HOME SETUPS OFF LEASH

Remember that your dog is a defensive, and not an offensive, weapon. You do not have the right to work offensively off leash like a police K-9 who may chase a fleeing suspect. However, when it comes to your property—your yard, house, car or boat—the dog is free to work off leash.

The situation setups in Level III protection will be more dramatic because we make it harder on the dog. It is up to the decoy to be creative—yell, use a starting pistol (dependent upon where you live) or any number of distractions.

198

Your setups can be more creative. For instance, the dog may be upstairs, totally unaware that the decoy has arrived. The decoy may barge into the house yelling and threatening assault. You can now see just how the dog will react. We also like to change decoys on dogs during this phase because it helps to add realism. You can let the dog in the house on a search and the decoy can bolt from a hiding place and attempt to run out the back door.

AUTOMOBILE PROTECTION

You can leave your dog in a parking lot in your car. The decoy can attempt to enter the car and take something off the seat. If you give it some thought, there are many situations that you can set up.

NOTE: It is imperative that you **be aware AT ALL TIMES of the safety of others and diplomacy with your neighbors.** Training sessions generally only last a few minutes. Reasonable people should be able to tolerate this.

Caution: Remember, dogs do not possess the ability to reason, they react largely on instinct and conditioned responses. Two things that can confuse a dog and elicit the wrong response follow:

1. People wearing ski clothing (i.e., parkas, ski suits, etc.) because they resemble bite suits. In general, this is not a problem but it is advisable to be aware.
2. People swinging sticks, bats, crutches or any object that could be construed as a weapon in the direction of a family member.

Avoiding these problems is part of awareness, which is most important to the K-9 owner/handler.

Dallas demonstrates a frontal muzzle attack on Pon. Muzzle attack teaches the dog to use his body like a lineman in football.

CHAPTER XVI

Advanced Protection

BY NOW, the dog has been in serious protection training for six months to one year and is probably one and a half to two years of age. The dog should be settling and becoming mature. Due to necessity, we have had to spend a lot of time using equipment with the dog for our safety. It is now time to bring the dog back on the decoy, intruder or agitator again.

MUZZLE ATTACKS

Purpose: To teach the dog to attack the decoy, not the equipment. To teach use of the dog's body to take the decoy down.

This requires a good German basket muzzle that costs approximately $100 to $200. *Do not try to use another kind of muzzle as this would be extremely dangerous.* The decoy should wear very rugged clothes that cover the body totally. The reason behind this is that the dog will scratch the person while the decoy is on the ground and this can be painful.

The muzzle must fit properly and you should pull at it yourself to ensure the muzzle cannot come off and the mouth cannot slip out.

The decoy agitates the dog as in civil defense work. The dog gets to a peak of intensity and the handler, on cue, lets the dog go to the end of the leash. The decoy, purposely off balance, should allow the

Using a firearm and shooting blanks gets the dog used to loud noises.

dog's weight to knock him down. Next, the decoy rolls onto his stomach and can either fight with the dog or attempt to pull away. Either will keep the dog's interest through Prey or Defense Drive. When sufficiently dominated, the decoy freezes and the dog is called "Out" and to "Heel."

It is our belief that the dog should hit like a football lineman. This should *not* resemble play. Rottweilers are especially good at this as are all of the Mastiff-type breeds. The Bullmastiff and the Dogue de Bordeaux, to name two, are excellent muzzle attack dogs. The muzzle attack can be accomplished at a distance. We prefer close-quarter muzzle attacks within 10 feet of the handler. This applies to protection and K-9 security work as it teaches the dog to use the whole body rather than just the mouth.

HIDDEN SLEEVES AND WEAPONS

Hidden sleeves add realism to window and door bites. The dog is biting an arm hidden under a typical street jacket. *It is the closest thing to a real bite the dog will ever get.* Weapons and the sounds they make also add realism. If the dog has been conditioned in advance to their sound you can now agitate and fire a blank gun at the same time.

Locations:

- In the car
- At doors
- Windows
- Sliding doors

Some dogs are too strong to do hidden sleeve work safely. This is a decision of the training director and the decoy.

AGILITY EXERCISES

You have practiced your Agility exercises in the past. Now we will use Agility in bite work. We have the dog scale the wall, or cross a catwalk on the way to a bite. Be creative and make things up. Use bales of straw, rows of chairs, slippery floors, plastic sheeting, water, or whatever you like. Every time your dog conquers a new obstacle, it will build confidence.

GUARDING OBJECTS

Teaching a dog to guard an object in reality only has its uses in security work. You can teach a dog to guard an object of your choice and it is fun to watch. In reality, you would never tell the dog to bite anyone who tried to pick up that object. This is what guarding the object is all about. If you had one million dollars in a briefcase it would come in handy.

The exercise is to teach the dog, for instance, to guard this valuable briefcase. Once the briefcase is set next to the dog and the dog is told to guard, it is understood that anyone other than the handler who attempts to reach for the briefcase will be bitten. If the person attempts to drag the dog away, the dog will *release the bite* within 10 to 15 feet of the briefcase *and return* to it.

POISON-PROOFING

Serious poison-proofing is done with shock. A sturdy fence charger like the type used for livestock has to be purchased. After it is set up and grounded, we attach a long wire with an alligator clip on the

Using obstacles teaches the dog to be versatile.

Teaching the dog to guard a briefcase has applications in security work.

end. Foil is attached and various foods are spread out on the foil. The food is randomly left in different locations and at different times of the day. The dog will learn that tasting it will result in being shocked, and will learn *not* to go near the food left on the ground.

You also need to have volunteers or your trainers hold the clip and attempt to feed the dog through the fence. For poison-proofing to work, you must not be in the habit of tidbitting your dog. If you feel you are at high risk, you should definitely do this. If you do not, it is strictly a personal decision.

CONVERSION TRAINING

Conversion training is the converting of a K-9 from one function to another, i.e., from Schutzhund to personal protection or from police work to personal protection. With any of these functions, the dog already understands all of the basics, and simply needs the gaps filled in between old and new functions. Many dogs purchased through importers need control work as well, especially from the threat command to the Out.

Typically, the focus of conversion training is on realistic situation setups around the house, property or anywhere that the dog will be expected to work. Teaching body bites on the European suit is also important so that the dog is confident in placing a bite wherever necessary. Conditioning is vital to the dog. A pup started in a European sport where the equipment is emphasized will always tend to be equipment-oriented.

Working without equipment is also important. Agitating over and around the equipment helps to focus the dog's attention on the person. The muzzle is also an effective tool during this portion of the dog's training.

A sizeable problem in conversion training is teaching a dog who for years has had nothing but sleeve work to bite the leg. For some dogs, this is a near impossible feat. Generally, if you use a tie out line and wear only the pants, you can teach the dog the leg bite. Eventually, the problem is that you will put on the jacket as well. The dog that is conditioned to the arm will look for it even while biting the leg. When given the chance, the dog will transfer to the arm.

Although the sport dog can be converted to personal protection training at three to four years of age, this dog will never be as proficient

Canto Vom Heilbenbōsch Sch. I, demonstrates how difficult it is to convert a Schutzhund dog from arms to legs.

Even with high kick he is focused on the sleeve.

CHAPTER XVII

European Sport, K-9 Home Security and Personal Protection

WHAT IS THE DIFFERENCE?

Dogs are being used today in many different ways. In work and in play, we have sought out the company and abilities of a K-9 companion. Within the contexts of the various jobs that K-9s perform, these are various terms that can be confusing to the novice. The tasks that a dog must perform in each job description are easily misunderstood.

Dogs are utilized by government, state and local agencies to assist in law enforcement. Their duties range from patrol, searches and tracking to narcotics and explosives detection. Dogs are also used for private security work with duties ranging from executive security to security patrol and business security.

On the home front, dogs are utilized as home companion and protection dogs. Some of these dogs accompany their owners to work and function as personal bodyguards at work and at home.

There are people who choose to pursue a hobby they can share with their dogs. Still other dogs are trained in Tracking and Agility,

Obedience and protection skills in order to compete in European sport such as Schutzhund, IPO, KNPV or Ring Sport.

One commonly asked question is what K-9 means. K-9 has become a recognized symbol representing the working dog, typically referring to a security, police or protection dog. In reality, K-9 is a code for canine (*canis*—Latin for dog). All dogs are canines. A perfect example of how terms have become confused follows. We are often asked if we train K-9s or how one becomes a K-9. Actually, this would be asking how to become a dog.

Many people believe that Schutzhund training is personal protection training. This is a common misconception due to the fact that many protection methods have been developed from Schutzhund techniques. Schutzhund dogs are also commonly converted to military, police or home protection services when they have finished competition.

With regard to military and police K-9s, people most often picture a patrol dog working with a human partner. Although this is one aspect of the police K-9, there are other descriptions that are equally important such as explosives and narcotics detection.

When business or property security is concerned, the typical person thinks of a dog snarling behind a fence with a danger sign affixed to it. The business security dog is just as likely to be found in the executive protection role, escorting the owner who is wearing a three-piece suit or quietly protecting the owner who is working in a business environment.

These are just some of the many stereotypes and misconceptions regarding protection K-9s. In order to clarify the training and job-related duties of each of these dogs, we have spoken to individual trainers and handlers in their respective fields. Each has provided us with insight in their field of expertise. We wish to sincerely thank these contributors for their insights.

EUROPEAN SPORT: SCHUTZHUND, IPO, FRENCH RING SPORT

European Dog Sport came into existence in Western Europe in the 1800s. Depending on the sport you are referring to, it is generally going to be one hundred to two hundred years old. Each of the sports involves various tests of the dog's working abilities including Tracking, Obedience, Agility and protection. Dog sport originated out of the desire to preserve the working abilities of German Shepherd Dogs and other working breeds.

Schutzhund—Use of German sleeve (Nana des Deux Pottois Sch. I, A.D. with David Macias).

Ring Sport—Use of French Ring suit (same dog; same decoy).

For instance, the German Shepherd (in Germany) cannot receive a V-Rating at a conformation show unless it has successfully passed a Schutzhund examination. The dog must compete in a conformation show for a V-Rating (excellent conformation) as well as have a minimum Schutzhund I, KKL I "A", AD and hip certification in order to qualify for the title of Sieger (champion) at a German show. The dog who cannot accomplish all of these prerequisites will not be recommended for breeding by the Kormeister (breed master). This process helps to limit the number of puppies born and ensures that the quality remains high on those that are produced.

IPO (International Pruefungsordnung)—Schutzhunds International form followed Schutzhund to this country. Schutzhund and IPO trials are held in conjunction with one another. French Ring Sport and its Netherland version—KNPV—did not arrive in this country until 1986. Stewart Hilliard and Charlie Bartholomew hosted the first Ring Sport seminar in Denver, Colorado. To date, French Ring Sport remains in its infantile stage with a few clubs scattered across the United States. French Ring and KNPV differ from Schutzhund and IPO in that they involve different tasks such as guarding objects, broad jumping and biting the legs of the full body suit. A very intricate sport to teach, it is a spectacle to watch. The Belgian Malinois is the dog of choice in French Ring and KNPV.

Due to limited space, we cannot cover all of the sports as we would like to. It would require another book to accomplish this. Therefore, we have chosen to concentrate on Schutzhund as it is currently the most popular of the dog sports in this country.

SCHUTZHUND

Schutzhund arrived in the United States in 1957. The late Gernot Riedel, a German immigrant who passed away in 1991, founded Schutzhund in this country.

In 1963, the Peninsula Canine Corps of Santa Clara, California, was organized. This club's membership consisted primarily of police officers. Due to overwhelming interest, the club soon opened its doors to the public as well. It wasn't until 1969 that the first SV (German Shepherd Dog Club of Germany)–sanctioned trial took place in Los Angeles, California. USA (United Schutzhund Clubs of America), formed in 1975, is the largest and most prestigious club in the United States today, boasting approximately twenty-five thousand members.

David Macias is currently the West Coast Regional Director of

Schutzhund.

Schutzhund USA. We asked David which breeds are accepted in Schutzhund trials. His response was, "In general, any breed that weighs fifty pounds or more that possesses a good nose for tracking, is capable of rigorous Obedience and has proper drives for protection work may compete."

Typical breeds:

- German Shepherd Dog
- Rottweiler
- Doberman Pinscher
- Belgium Malinois
- Belgian Sheepdog
- Belgian Tervuren
- Bouvier des Flandres
- Giant Schnauzer
- Airedale Terrier
- Other suitable breeds

Since David has worked extensively with Schutzhund, police and personal protection K-9s, we asked him to explain the difference as he sees them. He explained that Schutzhund, police narcotics and explosive detection dogs work primarily out of their Prey Drives. Their reward is to receive the prey object (i.e., sleeve, jute toy or ball). The patrol dog, who will meet up with the "bad guys" on the street, has to be higher in defense. Security and personal protection K-9s also require a higher level of Defensive Drive. This stands to reason since to unconditionally trust a stranger would render the protection K-9 ineffective.

Another significant difference that David pointed out is in testing. Given that each dog in its respective field is taken completely through training, who decides that the dog is qualified for the job?

The answer varies depending on the task. Schutzhund dogs are tested by a qualified judge and their scores are logged as a permanent record in the dog's score book. This is true with all other European sports as well.

Military and police K-9s are also required to pass tests. Military dogs are subject to regular testing throughout their service. Police K-9s are subject to P.O.S.T. Certification (Peace Officers Standards of Training of California).

Security and home protection dogs are not subjected to testing. The amount and style of training is decided by the dog's owner and the trainer employed by the owner. Because of this lack of testing, the quality of protection or security dogs differs greatly from dog to dog. The owner also plays a great part in this. A dog and trainer can work very well together. However, give the same dog to an inept or ambivalent owner and you cannot ensure how well the dog will work. You also cannot guarantee that the owner will ever work the dog.

David indicated that he would like to see some type of standard testing procedure established for protection and security dogs. We have been saying this for years. It is desirable to force compliance to a standard as this would prevent certain people from training dogs without Obedience and control as an integral part of their system. It also hopefully would make the point to owners that this is a serious business that they cannot take lightly.

One of the problems that exists within the protection training industry today is trainers who provide protection work without the requirement of Obedience. Fortunately, these types of trainers are in the minority. Any dog trained in this manner is a danger to everyone concerned, including the owner. This is why BH (European Obedience title) is required before the Schutzhund I.

Having been involved with European sport throughout the years, we asked David how much of a problem he has encountered with people looking at Schutzhund as an inexpensive means to protection train a dog. This is a common problem for sport clubs since memberships costs approximate $200 to $250 per year. People view this as inexpensive compared to private trainers' fees which can mount up to four to five times this much a year.

David screens people from the start. "I ask them if they want to compete for titles or if they want a personal protection dog. They generally do not know what I am asking and they will answer honestly. Most of these will want personal protection, so I recommend a licensed trainer. To the rest, I explain that Schutzhund is a sport that requires dedication. You must train four to five times per week consistently and two or three times a week with the club. You must practice all of the skills in Tracking, Obedience and protection. If you are not in the sport to compete, you will be wasting the club's time, as competition is the purpose. Members are not immediately accepted. They have a probation period where the club will judge the commitment of the member and then vote on their application for membership. This is not a personal protection club."

If they are truly interested in competition, this will not discourage them.

Deputy Johnson and his K-9 partner Ricky.

DRIVE WORK

To further explain the major difference between European Dog Sport and reality-based protection training, we must look at the drive work. When the dog works in the Prey Drive, as is taught in European sport, the dog is chasing and biting at the prey object (the equipment sleeve or suit) for fun and reward.

In the wild, a good example of Prey Drive is when a wolf chases prey (a rabbit, etc.). Defensive Drive is shown when a wolf defends the den from unwanted intruders.

David explains that this is very much like practicing Katas in martial arts. If you take the sleeve off and throw it to the side, the sport dog will go for the sleeve and is therefore practicing all of the moves without the true intent of bodily harm to the agitator.

The police, patrol, security or home protection dog is trained through the same procedures. However, the main focus is on doing battle with the agitator. When the dog has finished training, the equipment will be spit out and the dog will keep coming at the main target—the agitator.

A dog is taught to expect the unexpected as anything goes on the street. The person may attack, yell, scream and/or hit the dog with various objects. It is for this reason that a trainer works at making a dog streetwise.

In European sport the same exercise is repeated over and over again until the dog understands exactly what to expect. The sport dog is also worked on a training field where the environment remains consistent. Police and security K-9s are subjected to various environments dependent on their duty assignment. The asset for the homeowner is that the protection dog works in his or her own territory. There is a natural instinct to protect here, where the dog is comfortable and knows every square inch of the area.

This should not be misunderstood to mean that a dog only works in one drive. In order to get a balanced response in training, you must work the dog in both drives. The best sport dogs have a natural tendency to be higher in Prey Drive and are worked more in Prey Drive. Conversely, personal protection and patrol dogs should be higher in defense and worked more toward the Defensive Drive.

HOME AND PERSONAL PROTECTION

There are many different uses for the home and personal protection dog. This dog will guard home and family with his life. Lifestyle has a lot to do with how much protection the dog can render. It stands to reason that a dog cannot protect you when not with you.

In the area of home and personal protection, the dog has three primary functions:

1. Grounds protection (outside parameter)
2. Family protection (in the house)
3. Personal protector (with owner)

ESTATE PROTECTION

For those with large investments in their property and furnishings, security has become a necessity. In a few minutes a thief can carry out valuables worth hundreds of thousands of dollars with little or no risk of personal harm in situations with no dogs or protection devices.

This is where the estate protection K-9 is an asset. Again, it is a necessity to post signs at all entrances to the property. This works as

Linda Schlax relies on Sheeba to help protect her in her business.

a deterrent as well as a warning to workers entering the property. The estate protection dog's primary function is to deter people from entering the property without the owner's consent. The area between the gate and the home is guarded. At the owner's discretion, the dog may also function as a home and personal protection dog when kept in the house or with the owner on a leash.

It is wise to poison-proof the dog who is going to guard an estate. Poison is one way to get past a dog, so the protection dog should be taught not to accept food from anyone but the owner. There are three effective ways of doing this that are covered in chapters XI and XVI. Agitating the dog while offering food is also effective as the dog will identify any offer from outside the fence as an aggressive act.

Throughout the past ten years, Ms. Joan Stone has had protection dogs trained for her estate and personal protection. Her most recent purchase was a two-year-old male Rottweiler. In explaining why having a protection dog is important to her, she says, ''You get used to

218

It's nice to have eyes in the back of your head.

the sense of security with having the dog around. When you lose your dog, you feel vulnerable again. I don't like that feeling. I always want my dog nearby.''

HOME PROTECTION

In your home the dog has the advantage of knowing the territory well. Your dog is familiar with the particular noises and smells of your home and can detect strange noises and smells that may be associated with an intruder. The wise owner of the protection dog will have a preset plan should the K-9 be alerted to a prowler. The owner may choose to get a weapon, or remain secure in a locked safe room with a telephone.

Whatever the plan, the owner and dog are a team that sticks together. If it comes down to being backed into one room together, the dog makes the first attack on entry, thereby giving the human partner a few precious seconds to take action. This is not the kind of situation anyone desires to be in, but imagine the disadvantage if you do not have the dog to alert and defend you.

PERSONAL PROTECTION

The same dog that protects the estate or home can also provide personal protection on late-night shopping trips or to the local bank ATM. There are automatic door openers that work on remote for those who want the security of knowing the dog can be released from the car in the advent of an assault.

For joggers and cyclists, some of the more agile breeds make fantastic companions. The dog can offer you protection while you provide the dog with good exercise.

CHAPTER XVIII

Protection Dogs—
True Stories

THROUGHOUT THE YEARS, we have trained thousands of dogs and people. One of the exciting factors of this line of work is the unknown—you never know who or what lies ahead. Some of our clients are well-known celebrities, sports and political figures. It is interesting to get to know these people on a personal basis with their dogs as the focal point of our conversations. You learn a lot about a person's character when you deal with a member of their family.

You would be surprised at how different many celebrities are from their images. There are some that you would think were very caring people, who in reality are very uncaring toward their animals (they treat them as if they are stage props to be added and discarded at will). Others possessing the most violent reputations care very deeply about their animals.

One of the most amusing aspects of our job is protection training. With this type of training, you have the chance to yell and scream and really let your frustrations out. Everyone has a good time! We are proud of the fact that in the thirteen years since we have been in business, our dogs have circumvented many incidents of crime or violence, but we have yet to hear of any unwarranted bites. It makes us feel good when we are helping people to feel more secure.

A number of the stories that have been passed on to us have been

Beau

interesting and have proven to us that training does pay off. We would like to share some of these stories with you.

BEAU—GERMAN SHEPHERD DOG, MALE

Beau's owners saw protection training demonstrated on a television talk show. They promptly decided that this was what they wanted Beau to be like. They arranged for training to begin. Beau was the typical nine-month-old Shepherd whose feet were too big for the rest of the body. Following a year of training, Beau soon grew into his feet and matured into an excellent dog.

One night, while working situation setups at their residence, it was noticed that Beau could open windows. There were decoys at the windows when suddenly he shoved the window open and attempted to jump out at them. It was learned that the children had been sneaking Beau into their room at night by letting him jump into the window at bedtime and out the next morning. Beau soon learned to work the window with his nose.

One Fourth of July (following Beau's Level 3 protection training), the family left home. Beau was in the backyard. An intruder attempted to avoid Beau by going into the house from the front. Beau realized that someone was in the house and ran to the childrens' window, opened it with his nose and jumped in. The best that anyone could tell, Beau must have scared the intruder to death. Tables were overturned, articles were strewn across the floor, the French doors leading into the backyard were wide open and there was a small piece of bloody denim material by the back fence.

LADY—ROTTWEILER, FEMALE

Lady lived in an old mansion with her twenty-year-old owner and her mother. A few months previously, Lady had been through Obedience and Level 1 protection training.

One night, Lady's young owner was in her bedroom preparing to retire. Lady suddenly ran to the door and began whining and scratching at it. Her owner let her out and followed her downstairs. Lady ran straight to the laundry room door and, after putting her nose to the crack in the door, began barking aggressively. Her owner was reminded of the Check command she had practiced and promptly called the police. When the officers arrived, they brought out three teenage boys who claimed they thought the house was abandoned. This was not a very believable story since there were cars in the driveway, the house was fully furnished and the lights were on.

MAGNUM—DOBERMAN PINSCHER, MALE

Magnum was purchased by a young executive couple. He had been through Obedience and Level 1 protection training.

One night, his owner was walking him through the couple's complex. Someone suddenly came running past them. Magnum turned to see police officers chasing an intruder. Magnum lunged after the fleeing man so the owner quickly decided to let the dog go. Magnum caught up with the intruder, turned and executed a bark and hold. The police caught up and Magnum was retrieved by his owner. The bad guy had assumed the dog was a police K-9 and was quite surprised to find out that the dog was someone's personal pet.

We repeated this story later to Greg, a client of ours who is a police officer. A few weeks later, Greg was involved in chasing an alleged rapist the department had been after for weeks. This perpetrator was nicknamed the "track star" because no one could catch him. Greg was chasing the man and knew he had no chance of catching up. He yelled, "Stop, or I'll send the dog!" The bad guy instantly froze and put his hands up. While being handcuffed, the man asked Greg, "Where's the dog?" Greg calmly responded, "I lied."

KNUCKLEHEAD—DOBIE/COLLIE/VIZSLA MIX, MALE

A very unusual looking dog, when agitated Knucklehead would literally stand on his toenails. The owner, a groomer, used to take the dog everywhere she went. During training, car agitation was worked on extensively as Knucklehead was always in it. It got to be a joke to see if anyone could sneak up on him while he slept peacefully in the backseat. When Knucklehead would see the people and go off, the entire car would shake.

One night after work, the owner stopped to get a pizza. When she came out, a van full of teens was sitting next to her car. She put the pizza in the car and proceeded into a convenience store to purchase a soft drink. As she was coming out she saw a young male reaching into her car for the pizza. Just as she realized what she was seeing, she saw Knucklehead spring from the backseat and grab the guy by the shoulder. The youth screamed, dropped the pizza, jumped into the van and sped away. Guess what Knucklehead ate for dinner that night?

SHARA—ROTTWEILER, FEMALE

Shara's owners wanted a protection dog after they were held at gunpoint in their own home by gang members who knew they had a

Knucklehead

safe in the house. They decided to get a dog for a companion as well as for protection. No further incidents occurred at their home.

In time, they bought a new business and Shara began riding to work with the husband every day. One day, on the way home, Shara's owner was being harassed by youths who appeared to be gang members. He was especially worried because his seven-year-old niece was with him. Trying to put some space between his van and the other car, he had to stop at some railroad tracks when a train was crossing. As he looked in the rearview mirror, a youth from the car got out and started coming toward the van.

Taking the offense, the owner exited the van with Shara and faced the oncoming youth, who was now flanked by two more. As soon as the other two saw the dog, they stopped in their tracks. The leader

Janco

came a little closer and dared, "Go ahead, tell her to bite me." Shara's owner responded, "You keep coming at me, and then I'll tell her to bite you." The leader gave that some thought and decided to get back into his car. This was a case where the mere presence of the dog was all that was needed.

JANCO—BELGIAN MALINOIS, MALE (LAPD)

Janco, a police dog, was imported from Holland. He was one of the only dogs I have met who could make the hair raise on the back of my neck. He had been a rebel in Europe. Although he was an awesome patrol dog who was all business, he refused to wear a muzzle. By the time he was checked out for a K-9 security agency, he had been in and out of three different police departments. The officers were all intimidated by him and it was no wonder, you could sense that he was on edge and sharp as a knife.

One night, after working with him, the trainer entered his kennel with a bowl of food. Three others were on the outside of the kennel. The dog suddenly ran at the trainer and performed a bark and hold. Another trainer outside banged on the kennel, distracting Janco long enough for the first trainer to escape. He rushed to the door and the trainer closed it just as Janco hit it. Needless to say, it was decided that the dog was too much for what was needed. He belonged in a combat zone.

Janco's next "owner" was the LAPD. He was matched up with a six-foot three-inch Vietnam combat veteran who had a similar disposition. The two were patrolling in South Central Los Angeles when they were attacked in an alley one night by a gang. The dog took down three men before he was killed with a shotgun. His partner was shot in the shoulder, but survived. Janco had done his job—he took the shot that could have killed his handler. Janco died a hero in South Central Los Angeles in 1989.

A picture of mutual respect and affection; two important ingredients in the coexistence of people and dogs.

CHAPTER XIX

Conclusion

HUMANS AND DOGS have coexisted and lived together for thousands of years. In the beginning, dogs were used primarily for hunting and guarding purposes. A dog literally helped put food on the table and would then help protect the family and their property from unwanted intruders.

Thousands of years later, we are still using dogs for the same purposes. The difference lies in the fact that throughout the years, we have learned how to communicate better with our K-9 companions. This has served to broaden our abilities to teach them various skills.

We can truly celebrate the fact that we have grown in our capacity to appreciate the K-9's unique abilities. Dogs are now involved with us at every level of our existence from the government (i.e., war, military, police) to the private sector (i.e., executive/VIP security, home and personal protection).

Today's family has the ability to add the protection K-9 to their security options. When selected, cared for and trained properly, a dog will not only provide a sense of security, but will also give love, companionship and unconditioned loyalty, rare qualities in today's world.

Appendix

AKC and European Sport Titles

AKC (AMERICAN KENNEL CLUB) TITLES

CH.	AKC Conformation Title of Champion
Int. CH.	International Champion
OTCH.	Obedience Trial Champion
CD	Companion Dog Title—First level AKC title
CDX	Companion Dog Excellent Title—AKC Intermediate Title
UD	Utility Dog Title—AKC Advanced Obedience Title
TD	Tracking Degree awarded by AKC
TDX	Tracking Dog Excellent Degree awarded by AKC— Roughly equivalent to FH
OFA	(Orthopedic Foundation for Animals) Certifies the hips of a prospective breeding animal—ACCEPTABLE RATINGS: FAIR, GOOD, EXCELLENT

EUROPEAN TITLES

"A" STAMP	German Hip Rating for breeding suitability
DVG	German Alliance for Utility Dog Sports

VA	(Select) Show Rating given at Sieger Show
V	(Excellent) Show or Performance Rating
SG	(Very Good) Show or Performance Rating
G	Good
B	Satisfactory
M	Insufficient
U	Unsatisfactory
Korung	Breed Survey (not a title)
KKL I	Excellent—Recommended for Breeding
KKL II	Minor fault, but still suitable for breeding
ZTP	Breed Suitability test, involving basic Obedience, Protection and Conformation evaluation
Sch. I, II, III	German Dog Sport involving Obedience, Tracking and Protection skills
IPO I, II, III	International equivalent to Shutzhund
BR	French Ring Brevet—Beginning degree
FR I, II, III	French Ring degrees for Obedience, Agility and Protection
KNPV I, II, III	Netherlands degrees for Obedience, Agility and Protection
AD	Endurance Title—12-mile run
FH	Advanced Tracking title
BH	Traffic Control Dog
WH	Watch Dog
DPO	Police Dog
HGH	Herding Dog

Suggested Reading

Barwig, Susan, and Stewart Hilliard. *Schutzhund—Theory and Training Methods*. New York: Howell Book House, 1991.

Bamberger, Michelle, DVM. *Help! A Quick Guide to First Aid for your Dog*. New York: Howell Book House, 1993.

Campbell, Dr. William. *Behavior Problems in Dogs*. Santa Barbara, CA: American Veterinary Publications, Inc., 1991.

Carlson, Delbert G., DVM, and James M. Giffen, MD. *Dog Owner's Home Veterinary Handbook*. New York: Howell Book House, 1992.

Fox, Michael. *Understanding Your Dog*. New York: Coward, McCann, and Geoghegan, 1992.

Pfaffenberger, Clarence. *The New Knowledge of Dog Behavior*. New York: Howell Book House, 1963.

Lanting, Fred L. *Canine Hip Dysplasia*. Loveland, CO: Alpine Publications, Inc.

Saunders, Blanche. *The Complete Book of Dog Obedience*. New York: Howell Book House, 1978.

Strickland, Winifred. *Expert Obedience Training for Dogs*. New York: Macmillan Publishing, 1988.

Whitney, Leon, DVM. *Dog Psychology*. New York: Howell Book House, 1971.

Glossary of Terms

AGITATE/AGITATION: Bringing out the dog's courage, defense, and prey drives at the appropriate times.

AGITATION STICK: A stick made of nylon, padded or nonpadded, bamboo reed, whip, or popper. It can be used to make noise or to lightly tap the dog in training.

AKC SHOW: American Kennel Club show, typically involving Conformation or Obedience. Tracking, herding, and coursing events are also available.

BASIC OBEDIENCE COMMANDS: Heel, Sit, Down, Come and Stay, learned both on and off leash.

BITE COMMAND: Command to apprehend a person. "Fass" in German.

CHAMPION DOG: A dog that through competition in the breed ring has earned enough points to be named a champion.

CHECK COMMAND: Command to check the house or search for intruders.

CHOKE CHAIN/TRAINING COLLAR: Collar that constricts around the neck when a correction is applied and releases to a loose position when the dog is correctly under command.

CONFORMATION: The anatomical makeup of the dog judged for correctness of structure and type according to a breed Standard.

CONTROLLED AGGRESSION: The act of making the dog aggressive but **NOT** mean (Obedient aggression). At the same time teaching to cease aggression on command.

DEFENSE DRIVE: The drive to protect territory, self, owner, or property.

DESENSITIZED: To lessen sensitivity through experience.

EUROPEAN BITE SUIT: The full body suit designed in Europe for maximum movement with maximum protection for the decoy.

FEAR AGGRESSIVE: A dog that is aggressive because he/she is afraid. The dog shows the body language of fear, i.e., tail tucked, eyes rolled back, hackles up, etc., while acting aggressive.

FETCH: To retrieve an article.

"GIB LAUT": Speak command. German command to bark.

HANDLER: The person who holds the dog and coaches the dog into the proper actions.

HIP DYSPLASIA: A primarily genetic disorder in the ball and socket of the hip joint that can result in crippling the dog.

HOLD COMMAND: Command to guard the person silently or with a bark and hold.

LIGHT LEASH: A light Toy breed leash.

LONG LINE: 30-foot leash.

MUZZLE: A device worn on the face that will not allow the dog to bite.

OUT COMMAND: Command used to cease aggression whenever necessary. The dog must obey the owner and remain calm.

PARVOVIRUS: An intestinal virus that is potentially fatal.

PET QUALITY: A pup or adult that because of one or more faults or deviations from the Standard should not be bred.

POLICE COLLAR: Two-inch (2″) wide leather collar used for protection.

PREY DRIVE: The drive that causes the dog to chase and bite at prey.

PRONG COLLAR: Collar that pinches neck at several points.

PUPPY GATE/BABY GATE: Gate used in doorways to hold or keep the pup out of a specific area.

PUPPY TUG: A device made of rolled burlap used to teach the dog to bite properly through play.

RECESSIVE GENES: Inherited characteristics that are not obvious in a given dog, but that may be passed on to offspring.

RING SPORT: French dog sport involving Obedience, Agility, and protection exercises.

SAFETY COLLAR: An extra collar worn in case equipment breaks.

SCHUTZHUND: German dog sport involving Obedience, Tracking and protection exercises.

SLEEVES: Protection equipment worn on the arm only. Used to teach the dog to bite with a full mouth.

SOCIALIZATION: Making sure that the dog is comfortable around adults, children, and other animals.

STAND COMMAND: Teaching the dog to stand for examination for practical purposes, Obedience, or show.

TAB/HANDLE: A 6–10-inch leash or handle.

TITLED: A degree earned through competition in a specifically regulated activity.

TRAINING DIRECTOR: The most knowledgeable person who directs the action between the decoy, handler and dog.

VON WILLEBRAND'S DISEASE: A free-bleeding disorder that is inherited.

"WATCH 'EM" OR "PAS-AUF" COMMAND: Command to dog to be alert.

ABOUT THE AUTHORS

George and Karen Duet own and operate Kingsden's Kennel and K-9 Companions Dog Training Co. Together with their associates and training staff they provide training for all breeds in problem-solving, Obedience and home manners. They specialize in training dogs of sound temperament in the art of personal protection and home and business security. K-9 Companions has branches in Los Angeles, Orange County, Riverside, and San Diego, California.

The Duets' backgrounds include experience in American Kennel Club Obedience Trials and conformation shows, German Schutzhund and French Ring Sport training, as well as U.S. Army training. George Duet retired from the Army after 20 years' service, and spent time as Kennel Master in Fort Benning, Georgia, and now also teaches the use of firearms to men and women. He is a distinguished pistol shot and was the Chief Sniper Instructor for the U.S. Army in Vietnam as well as the coach of the U.S. Army Shooting team, pistol division.

The Duets also provide protective services for VIPs in the form of handler-dog teams or protective agents on an on-call basis. They both hold the title of Personal Protection Specialist (P.P.S.) awarded by the Executive Protection Institute, Berryville, Virginia. They are members of Nine Lives Associates, an international network of personal protection specialists and are pioneering the field of K-9 security in the role of executive protection and estate protection.

The Duets are working with trainers and breeders to educate the public in K-9 management and training. They believe with proper breeding and training regulations, unwarranted attacks by all dogs can be drastically reduced.